Praise for *T*

"This book, *The Happy Heretic*, makes so much sense, and yet it turns traditional religious thinking and spirituality upside down. It is transformational in that it clearly explains the core issues of religious codependency, giving examples from our everyday lives and, in this way, creates a new understanding of our relationship with God. Nothing is left off the table.

"Leo has courageously argued what most of us have secretly known for years: God is not codependent. God does not fix or rescue us in times of tribulation and suffering. God is not needy for our attention. Rather, God is a *partner* in the living of life.

"*The Happy Heretic* confronts toxic religious messages and brings a spiritual awareness that affirms human possibility and responsibility. It's a great read."

—John Bradshaw, Author,
TV Personality, Mentor, Innovator, Philosopher,
Counselor, Theologian, Educator, and Elder

The Happy Heretic

Other Books by Leo Booth

The Angel and the Frog
Spirituality and Recovery
The Wisdom of Letting Go
Say Yes to Your Life
Say Yes to Your Spirit
Say Yes to Your Sexual Healing

The Happy Heretic

Seven Spiritual Insights for Healing Religious Codependency

Dancing with Pelagius and Rumi

Leo Booth

Health Communications, Inc.
Deerfield Beach, Florida
www.hcibooks.com

Library of Congress Cataloging-in-Publication Data

Booth, Leo, 1946-
The happy heretic : seven spiritual insights for healing religious
   codependency : dancing with Pelagius and Rumi / Leo Booth.
      p. cm.
   ISBN-13: 978-0-7573-1706-4 (pbk.)
   ISBN-10: 0-7573-1706-5 (pbk.)
   ISBN-13: 978-0-7573-1707-1 (e-pub)
   ISBN-10: 0-7573-1707-3 (e-pub)
1. Spirituality.   2. Spiritual life.   3. Meditations.   4. Codependency—
Religious aspects.   5. Pelagius.   6. Jalal al-Din Rumi, Maulana,
1207-1273.   I. Title.
   BL624.B6188 2012
   204'.4—dc23

                                                           2012034278

©2012 Leo Booth

All rights reserved. Printed in the United States of America. No
part of this publication may be reproduced, stored in a retrieval
system, or transmitted in any form or by any means, electronic,
mechanical, photocopying, recording, or otherwise, without the
written permission of the publisher.

HCI, its logos, and marks are trademarks of Health Communications, Inc.

Publisher: Health Communications, Inc.
         3201 S.W. 15th Street
         Deerfield Beach, FL 33442–8190

Cover design by Dane Wesolko
Interior Design and Formatting by Dawn Von Strolley Grove

Contents

Introduction

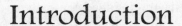

I'm a heretic!

I never thought in my wildest dreams that I would ever make this statement. I mean *me* saying it. Sure, others have said it about me for years, but now I'm saying it. And it feels good. Indeed, it feels *right*.

Now I'm on my journey. I thought it started when I was at theological college, studying the arguments between Saint Augustine of Hippo and Pelagius, but maybe it started earlier when I was a teenager and was introduced to Jabal-al-Din Rumi, known to the world as Rumi.

Rumi was a Muslim, a thirteenth-century poet who believed that divinity is *within* nature, as well as outside it, and he expressed his celebration of life with dance. His poetry made ideas come alive; divinity was made real. With Rumi, it is always a journey beyond words into ideas, and we never know where these ideas will take us. For me, it would take me beyond religious dogma into metaphysics, beyond belief into experience.

In a sense, we are all on a journey toward God, and because we have different ideas and experiences, our paths will be ever-changing. Rumi expressed his point of view in challenging poetry:

> Where am I going on this glamorous Journey?
> To your house, of course.
>
> (From *Love Poems from God* by Daniel Ladinsky)

This was also the message of Pelagius, a monk who was living around the fourth century, who was less poetic, yet who wanted to emphasize the *potential* perfection of the human being. When Pelagius was in Rome, he reacted against Augustine's theology that made all of man's activities dependent on God' grace. Augustine seemed to leave no place for human choice and moral responsibility. Pelagius believed that Augustine's doctrine of grace was a threat to human freedom. In a similar way, Rumi suggested that through imagination we not only experience the divine, but we express it. Pelagius, theologically, suggested the same. That's why below the title on the cover of this book it reads both "Seven Spiritual Insights for Healing Religious Codependency" and "Dancing with Pelagius and Rumi."

My journey into this heretical dance has taken years and is the culmination of many experiences: my flirtation with Catholicism as a young man, followed by theological training in Great Britain for the Anglican Church, ordination in the Church of England, and transferring into the Episcopal Church when I moved to the United States. Today, I'm an ordained minister in Unity of Christianity, a metaphysical church. But truth to tell, I'm a Pelagian. I'm a heretic. And I'm happy.

If I reflect upon the changing beliefs I've made in my life, they revolve around my disinterest with church dogma and my growing fascination with how the divine cocreates with nature. It wasn't a conscious formulation, as I'm presenting in this book, but rather a feeling that an exclusive preoccupation with what God is doing in our lives can take us away from realizing the human response. It increasingly seemed that the prayers I recited and the sermons I heard didn't fit with what I was actually experiencing and believed. I developed a growing agnosticism with "churchianity."

During this time I was reintroduced to the writings of Rumi. I had read Rumi as a young man, loving his energy and passion; however, in preparing for theological college, I had put aside his poems. And yet Rumi, for me, intuitively sensed that the mystical union of the physical with the divine could never fit a rigid formula—hence the concept of *whirling dervishes*. Rumi believed that in the fast dancing in circles we create a trance, a form of meditation, where the spirit of the person leaves the body and connects with the Divine. The whirling dervish becomes like a physical chant, and in the dance, God is experienced. Words and ideas come alive in physical expression because they existed within creation; the Creator lives in and through creation.

With these ideas whirling around in my mind, I found myself being involved in a series of questions concerning the relationship between spirituality and religion. Is there a difference between the two? Can you be spiritual without being religious? Could it be that spirituality is that mystical thread that unites the peoples of the world, regardless of religion or culture? What is the connection between divinity and humanity? Researching the teachings of Pelagius and rereading Rumi have enabled me to answer, for myself, some of these questions and have also given me a more dynamic understanding of spirituality.

Am I a Christian? Yes. But I'm more. Religion as an organization interests me little. I'm much more interested in a comprehensive spirituality that can be found in everything, the light and the darkness, the beautiful and the blemished, the sacred and the secular. Collectively, they make for the *mysterium tremendum*—the overwhelming mystery.

Now I'm able to understand these powerful words of Rumi:

> In your light I learn how to love.
> In your beauty, how to make poems.
> You dance inside my chest,
> where no one sees you,
> but sometimes I do,
> and that sight becomes this art.
> (From *Rumi: The Book of Love* by Coleman Barks)

The difference between this book and my previous

publications is clear. I'm a different person, and I've come to understand that the theology of Pelagius and the poems of Rumi have been percolating in my writings for years.

My first book was *Spirituality and Recovery*. The subtitle was *Walking on Water*. I can imagine a potential reader, seeing this subtitle, saying, "Why, the audacity of the man! He says he can walk on water. Who does he think he is, Jesus Christ?" Well, in a sense, yes. I had slowly come to believe that the spiritual power that was being demonstrated through Jesus is also available within you and me. I'm affirming what Pelagius said in the fourth century: "A man is able, if he likes, to be without sin."

This quotation challenges the message that has been around from the earliest times: *we are not perfect*. Everyone is flawed. We are not God. However, this did not stop Pelagius from asking the question, "But could we be perfect? Is it possible to live the life that Jesus lived?" Jesus seemed to imply this possibility when He said, "Greater things than I have done, you will do" (John 14:12).

It's undeniably true that if we keep hearing something, continually say it to each other, see it written in spiritual writings, then we come to believe it. Pelagius dared to think differently and considered the *possibility* that we were born perfect and under the right circumstances could remain perfect.

Let's take a moment to look at what is known about Pelagius. He was born around 354 AD in Wales, Britain. He was educated in both Greek and Latin, a monk but not a cleric; he was never an ordained priest. In his early years, he was admired by no less a person than Augustine of Hippo, who called him "a saintly man." When he moved to Rome, he became concerned about the moral laxity in the city, believing it was partly the result of Augustine's teaching concerning *divine grace*. Pelagius was concerned about the emphasis that Augustine placed upon God's grace—the idea that since the Fall of Adam, every good thought or action was dependent upon God. We could do nothing on our own. There was no teaching that affirmed the need for our response. There was little teaching concerning human responsibility; that we need to be accountable for our behavior. He was particularly disturbed by a famous quotation from Augustine, "Give me what you command and command what you will."

Pelagius believed that this saying discounted free

will, turning man into a mere automaton. He soon
became a critic of Augustine, disagreeing with him
concerning original sin and the working of God's
grace in perfecting salvation. Pelagius argued that if
human beings could discipline themselves in the way
exemplified by Jesus, then they could remain perfect.
He believed that grace needed to be connected with
human choice. Pelagius's personal discipline made
him extremely puritanical, teaching a strict regimen
to his disciples in order to ensure moral purity.

Pelagius was politically sensitive to the church of his
day, and yet he was gently rebelling, carefully challenging
its teachings. He affirmed the divine power that existed
within the church, but he also suggested a comprehensive
spirituality that was reflected in every human being—
even those who were born before the time of Jesus.

The church hierarchy ultimately supported the
theological arguments of Augustine, and Pelagius was
denounced as a heretic at the Council of Carthage in
418 AD. It is believed that Pelagius died of natural
causes in Palestine around 420 AD.

After studying the theological arguments that Pelagius had with Augustine, I became acutely aware that
they were both extremely scrupulous, often focusing

on the intrinsic meaning of one word or sentence. Their arguments seemed pedantic and petty, the very antithesis of the poetic writings of Rumi, and yet I clearly see emerging in Pelagius's teachings the seeds of Rumi's poetry and what today we call New Age or metaphysical thinking.

In this book I make reference to noetic science. It is not a new science; however, the focus of its research has been kept a secret from the general public. A few men and women in history expressed this discipline, but it never became a part of popular philosophical thinking until recently. The word *noetic* comes from the Greek word *nous,* which does not have an exact English translation but refers to an *inner knowing*, an intuitive perception that is beyond our natural senses or powers of reasoning.

In his popular book *The Lost Symbol*, the fiction writer Dan Brown alludes to noetic science and connects it with the untapped potential of the human mind. He suggests that human thought and energy influence the physical world, that the mysticism and philosophies of the past are connected with the scientific insights of the present.

Pelagius also had an understanding of this divine

relationship that we desperately need to manifest today. For the past twenty years, since being introduced to the metaphysical churches in America, I had often thought about Pelagius. In Unity of Christianity and other metaphysical churches we hear the following teachings: *Wherever we are, God is, and all is well;* every human being is born with an original blessing rather than original sin; we are children of God who can manifest divine attributes. However, it was after reading Dan Brown's book that I knew I needed to write this book.

I have called the following chapters Insights. Why? Because each section gives a powerful idea or concept that is different from traditional Christian teaching. Also, each of these insights gives a deeper understanding of who we are in our relationship with God. That's why I suggest that this book *changes* everything.

INSIGHT ONE:
Living the Good Life

*"Whenever I have to speak on the subject
of moral institution and the conduct
of a holy life, it is my practice first
to demonstrate the power and quality
of human nature and to show
what it is capable of achieving."*

—From Pelagius's letter to Demetrius

There is a powerful difference between living and merely existing. It has been my experience that most of us are just muddling through; a case of getting through life, a mindless boredom that percolates throughout most of the day. People are existing, not living.

This used to be my reality. For many years, especially in the days before I became sober, time just slipped away. Alcoholic drinking was the cause. What people call a hangover was for me a profound disconnection; I couldn't think, feel, or enjoy physical pleasure. I would sit for hours in a zombie state,

11

and the days would pass by. I certainly wasn't living the good life.

There is a story about two fish that exemplifies this experience:

> *Two small, frightened fish were huddled together in the ocean, afraid to move. Out of a deep cave came a large, beautiful fish. The glittering fish was brimming over with confidence and began to swim past the two little fish with great force. The big fish noticed the shivering forms and turned to the two fish and asked, "Why stay huddled together? Why don't you swim out into the clear, glistening water?"*

> *The two little fish looked at each other, and then one of them said, "Where is the water?"*

This story highlights a problem that many people face. They are *in* life, and yet not living. You begin to live when you recognize your *potential*.

The two fish know they are missing something. They know deep inside they were not created to live in fear. They know that the magic of life is eluding them; yet they are unsure of how to get it. Where is the water of life?

The two fish became tragic observers. Fear does this to people; it freezes them. We become scared stiff. Petrified. Prisoners within ourselves. The fear of rejection. The fear of not being good enough. The fear of being too small. The feeling of not being smart. The fear of being the wrong color, race, or religion. These fears group together to keep us isolated.

This story represents the difference between existing and living. Existing is what the two little fish were doing. They seemed incapable of making things happen. They asked questions, rather than seeking the answers. They never *initiated* anything. Many people are living like the two fish. Why are we so afraid? Well, perhaps these fears are created by fearful messages we received as children, some of which have been around for centuries.

This is why I want to bring attention to this little-known philosopher Pelagius. He understood that once we know who we are and what we were created with, this awareness allows us to live the good life—a life free of that all-consuming fear. The fear and apathy in the story of the two fish are beautifully expressed by Rumi when he suggests that to be disconnected or unaware of this divine passion, existing rather than living, is to look like *a dead fish*.

With passion pray.
With passion work.
With passion make love.
With passion eat and drink and dance and play.
Why look like a dead fish in this ocean of God?
(From the book *Love Poems from God* by Daniel Ladinsky)

As we will see in the next Insight, an overemphasis upon sin, brokenness, or helplessness can easily
develop into a codependent neediness. What is codependency? It is a word that describes a series of behaviors or attitudes that create an unhealthy relationship.
Definitions and explanations of codependent behavior
often revolve around low self-esteem issues, a pathetic
clinging to another person, and controlling characteristics that could involve verbal abuse or violence.
These behaviors are based upon the fear that the other
person might leave, pull away, or refuse to do what we
want. This feeling of being damaged goods will prompt
us to seek from others what we think is lacking within
ourselves.

Pelagius in his writings gives theological reasons as
to where this neediness, this not feeling good enough,
might come from. If we are told we are born sinful; that

we can do nothing good without God's grace; God's son had to die that we might be redeemed and go to heaven; if, from childhood, we heard that God is everything and we are nothing, it's not difficult to comprehend why many people feel like damaged goods, living with low self-esteem. These teachings and beliefs create what I'm calling *religious codependency*.

Our sense of self is understood only in the context of being fallen creatures, since Adam and Eve's sin has tainted everyone. Being told that only through God's grace can we do any good deed made us pathetically needy, clinging to the hope that God indeed will save or redeem us. Remember, in Augustine's teaching, there is no mention of our involvement in God's grace. We take no responsibility for our thoughts and actions. Everything is about what God is doing or has done. In this book, I will give descriptions and situations that exemplify what I'm calling religious codependency, describing how we developed and reflect this unhealthy relationship with God.

In twelve-step programs, people are thinking that if they give everything over to God, including their thinking, they will stay sober. People are asking God in prayer to do what they should be doing or creating for themselves. Because of an excessive emphasis on sin, maybe experienced in childhood, some people live a life of misery. They feel they have nothing of value to contribute in society. And when they do something they should be proud of, they take no credit, testifying it came only through God's grace. When religious messages become toxic, then religious codependency is often the result.

I'm not sure if I coined the term *religious codependency,* but I've not heard or read anything about it; *now this described religious toxicity has a name.*

When I reflect upon the story of the two fish, I see that not so long ago I was waiting for something or someone to tell me what to do. I was waiting for instructions; I was waiting for the big fish to come into my life. *And God was my big fish.* For too many years, I waited for things to happen, rather than initiated what I needed. Like the two little fish, I was existing, not living.

Most messages are made toxic by an overemphasis; religious messages are made toxic by an emphasis on a half-truth. An essential ingredient is left out. What could be a powerful message is reduced to a lie. If we are told only what is in one hand and not told what is in the other, we are being cheated. Half the truth is a lie. For most of my life, I got the hand that told me God was powerful, judgmental, and all-knowing. Religious society proclaimed that I should fear the power of God and seek personal forgiveness in my religion. Christians were expected to be servants of God and, in gratitude, worship Him. This is also true for most Muslims, Jews, Buddhists, Hindus, and other religious groups.

I grew up with these religious lessons. Occasionally I was happy, but I never felt powerful. Indeed, if I dared to speak about my gifts, if there was even a whiff of self-esteem, I was condemned for being sinfully proud. *God was everything*; *I was nothing without His grace.*

Nobody told me what was in the other hand. Nobody suggested I needed to create, that I was given a brain to use, that miracles required my cooperation. For years, I would beat my chest in church saying, *mea culpa, I am not worthy.* These religious messages that suggested God is everything and I am nothing created an imbalance. I was being fed from only one hand.

WHAT IS RELIGIOUS CODEPENDENCY?

Most religious people are raised with the idea that they are completely dependent upon God for all their wants and needs. Saint Augustine suggested that we can do nothing good except through God's grace. The message was, "I, in myself, can do nothing; it is only through God's grace that I can perform good works."

This message became a central dogma in the church, and it affected everyone. The power of the church influenced most parts of the then-known world; even non-Christians came to believe that they were sinful, inadequate, damaged, and completely dependent upon God.

Pelagius felt uncomfortable with this teaching because he said it lacked balance. It affirmed only what God was doing; it didn't speak to our involvement. Don't we have a say in our lives? Where is free will? Where is choice?

Coelestius, a disciple of Pelagius, wrote: "Suppose that I want to bend my finger or to move my hand, to sit, to stand, to walk, to run to and fro, to spit, or to blow my nose, to perform the offices of nature; must the help of God be always indispensable to me?"

Religious codependency condemns us as sinful or arrogant if we list our achievements or indicate any good deeds. Being a partner with God, responding to His call to live the good life, is anathema to the religious codependent. And yet surely a key ingredient to living the spiritual life involves having self-esteem, being proud of who we are and what we have created in our lives. I'm affirming a healthy self-confidence, not arrogance.

BECOMING CREATIVE

Pelagius realized that he was swimming against the tide of church tradition; everything in church worship spoke about what God was doing in His world. And from this type of worship and religious instruction developed messages that are common throughout Christianity and in some other religions:

- If God wants you to have it, then it will happen.
- There, but for the grace of God, go I.
- When your time is up, God will take you home.
- What God has joined together let no man put asunder.

In *The Happy Heretic* we will consider what our part in the above messages is. We will discover what is to be found in the other hand. Let's examine these examples below:

If God wants you to have it, then it will happen.

I do not believe that we have a job, wife, car, or a college degree just because God wanted us to have them; *I'm convinced that we also did something*. We attended the interview with an excellent résumè, we got to know and love the woman who is now our wife, we saved for the car that we now own, and yes, we studied hard for our exams.

There, but for the grace of God, go I.

I always liked this saying until I began to think about it. Do I really want to suggest that we are not in prison, or homeless or drunk because God's grace *stopped* these tragedies from happening to us? Should we thank God that we're not like those we feel sorry for, or do we need to be proud about the circumstances, actions, or choices that prevented us from breaking the law, making our house payment, seeking therapy to maintain our sobriety. Our *choices* create success in life. And we are necessarily involved, even if we're not always conscious of it.

When your time is up, God will take you home.

This saying feels appropriate when we die at eighty, in a comfortable bed, with family around us. It does not feel so acceptable when our teenage son or daughter is killed by a drunk driver or dies as a young soldier in war. Are we seriously suggesting that God directed the drunk driver or created the war? Maybe it is better to say accidents happen and people die in circumstances that are truly tragic. Yes, we are grateful for the time we shared together, but it is not helpful to suggest that God had a hand in an untimely death.

The saying also conjures up a picture of God as a master puppeteer, pulling the strings of life and death.

What God has joined together let no man put asunder.

In any marriage, healthy or unhealthy, both people are involved. The choice to marry is made for many reasons and sometimes there are unrealistic expectations on both sides. However, *it is the two people who make their marriage work*. Yes, God is involved, but He does not magically keep the couple together.

It is also unacceptable, especially if abuse is involved, to invoke a promise made before God in order to keep a toxic relationship together.

GOD'S GRACE ABOUNDS

I believe that God is involved in everything and, using traditional language, His grace abounds.

However, I believe that we play an essential role in the living of our lives. We are able to live the good life when we know, on a spiritual level, that we make life worth living. Our decisions and choices determine success or tragedy. God doesn't *make* anyone happy, sad, successful, or loving. That's our job.

Isn't this the message of *The Secret?* The book by Rhonda Byrne and the movie it inspired, became incredibly popular because they suggested that the church, with the help of patriarchs and bishops, including Saint Augustine, had felt it necessary to keep a secret from the people: *that divine creativity exists in each of us.* It is hard to control people, or keep them in a subservient position, if they know that they are powerful. *It was therefore decided by the church hierarchy that regular people should be kept from ever knowing this truth.*

Nevertheless, once you discover this *secret* and understand the implications of this divine awareness, everything changes. For the spiritual seeker, nothing will ever be the same.

Abundance is also something that we create. A criticism of *The Secret* is that it tended to overemphasize money and the acquisition of material things. That being said, people still need to be reminded that they create wealth, prosperity, and success in their lives. Money is a creative energy that we generate and demonstrate; it doesn't grow on trees. Some people say that money isn't everything, and I agree. But it is *something*. If you seek a spiritual life that is associated with poverty, then that's what you will create. The same goes for those who seek a spiritual life associated with wealth. Personally, I'm with Mae West, "I've been rich and I've been poor, and rich is better!" A key resource for creating wealth is work. Most people create money by the work they do and the effort or creativity they put into it. When a winning personality is added to the mix, alongside having achieved the right credentials, then success in life is possible, bringing abundance.

Noetic science suggests that self-esteem affects the cells in our brain and our overall health. This demonstration of our will or divine energy does more than keep us healthy, it can take us beyond the five senses into incredible insights and experiences. With this information *the secret* is exposed.

Today, traditional beliefs are being challenged, the creativity of brain energy is being understood, and amazing possibilities are being realized in medicine and technology. A dynamic spirituality is transforming not only religion but also the world. Ordinary people are developing their divine skills and joining the ranks of Buddha, Jesus, Michelangelo, Dante, Francis Bacon, Thomas Jefferson, Sir Arthur Conan Doyle, and, yes, Pelagius and Rumi.

Scientifically, we are able to document that people with a positive attitude live happier and healthier lives. Studies show that prayer and meditation enhance our confidence and vitality, increasing the quality of life. What we once considered divine qualities are now part of the human experience.

Let's take a moment to look at three qualities involved in living the good life:

Quality 1—Taking Care of Our Bodies

Traditional religions deliver the message that we need to escape the body in order to discover holiness. Indeed, Saint Augustine argued that our bodies and planet Earth, after Adam and Eve's expulsion from the Garden of Eden, became sinful and fallen. Pelagius dared to suggest an alternative thesis:

"And lest, on the other hand, it should be thought to be nature's fault that some have been unrighteous, I shall use the evidence of the scripture, which everywhere lay upon sinners the heavy weight of the charge of having used their own will and do not excuse them for having acted only under constraint of nature."

—The Letters of Pelagius and His Followers

I'm with Pelagius. God created nature, and it is not sinful; it is our choices that create imperfection. Our bodies, regardless of Adam and Eve's fall from grace, are not sinful. We should respect and nurture what God has created.

More will be said about this later, but for the moment, if we are to create the good life, then we need to take care of our bodies. It is not vanity to shave, wash, eat healthily, exercise, have a massage, or get a manicure. It is an expression of gratitude for God's creation.

Does that make Pelagius a metrosexual? Hardly. However, we cannot embrace a holistic understanding of spirituality without enjoying our physical nature and the physicality of others. Hugs strengthen a relationship, a gentle kiss reassures the faint hearted, and a caress can be a much-needed expression of love. It is not sinful to appreciate the beauty of another.

Noel Coward, author and playwright, supposedly remarked to a friend, "Spirituality involves style!" And style requires physical attributes. When we see our physicality as an expression of spirituality, then sexuality and romance are taken to another level. That's why so many artists who often had their works condemned by the church as sinful knew they were experiencing and expressing something divine.

Quality 2—Taking Care of Our Minds

Most religious organizations reveal two inconsistent attitudes when it comes to the mind. On the one hand, they applaud the evolved thinking of scientists, theologians, philosophers, and artists. On the other hand, they have tended to condemn or resist new or radical thinking.

The problem with demanding obedience is that it can easily lead to stagnation and passivity. Often religious leaders want creative thinking on their terms, and the radical thinker becomes the rebel, often ostracized, occasionally condemned, as being corrupt. A man who experienced such condemnation, Oscar Wilde, remarked, "The worst vice of a fanatic is his sincerity."

Can we ever live or create the good life if we feel a need to suppress our affection for people we secretly admire? I was sharing this thought with a friend who told me that he had also discovered the poems of Rumi as a student. His father, a Bible-thumping Pentecostal, would not permit Rumi's books in the house. This led to my friend's developing secretive behavior, fearfully reading Rumi as his father slept.

Radical thinkers don't intentionally want to think differently; they simply do. They don't wake up and decide to challenge religious leaders, family, or close friends. The truth is that after study and reflection, they are unable to agree with what others are saying; they are being honest.

When we take care of our mind, we respect our thoughts and ideas. Not to be able to think, speak, or write forces us to live in a prison. And being a radical thinker does not mean we disrespect the thoughts of others; rather we learn to *respectfully disagree*.

Quality 3—Taking Care of Our Feelings

The behavioral health work I do at treatment centers reaffirms my belief that for most people, it is easier to say what we think than to share how we feel. Why?

Because many people were raised with the following messages:

- Keep your feelings to yourself.
- Don't let people see you cry.
- You are weak if you show your feelings.
- Show your love in action, not words.

Growing up in England I rarely heard parents telling their children how much they loved them. Usually a gentle tap on the head or shoulder was seen as an appropriate expression of affection. We just didn't talk about feelings.

And yet feelings are an essential expression of who we are. Can we really love somebody if we don't know how they feel? Can they love us if they don't know how we feel?

We fear expressing our feelings because they often make us vulnerable—appearing weak or needy. When we share our feelings, the inner self is revealed, that part of us that we tried to hide for years. When we share our feelings, we are made known. *This is who we are.*

Masks, boxes, and prisons are created, because we're afraid of people knowing who we are or what we feel. And, probably, the people we are hiding from feel the same. We begin to live the good life when we are able, without shame, to move beyond these masks, boxes, and prisons, expressing how we honestly feel.

THE GOOD LIFE IS DIVINE

The Rumi concept of dancing is important because it celebrates our body, mind, and feelings as the divine connection:

God is in me and I am in God.
I am in you and you are in me.
We all reflect God.
(From *Love Poems from God* by Daniel Ladinsky)

When we are living the good life we express and participate in the divine. We open ourselves to the divine demonstration that is being revealed, manifesting God's powerful presence. In this sense, we are dancing *with* and *in* God.

INSIGHT TWO:
We Are Perfect

> *"That newborn infants are in
> the same condition that Adam was in
> before he fell . . . That infants, even
> if they die unbaptized, have eternal life."*
>
> —Pelagius's letter to Augustine

> *"A man is able, if he likes, to be without sin."*
>
> —Pelagius

I said in the introduction to this book that I'm a heretic. This word has come to denote a person in theological error; however, the original Greek word *hairetikos* can also mean *choice* or *a thing chosen*. With this alternative in mind, I believe that Pelagius offered a different interpretation, an alternative choice, explaining how God's grace is manifested in this world.

The early church decided, for many reasons, to be dogmatic. It determined what was right, what we should believe, and what was wrong. Period.

However, this attitude only birthed more heresies and today, many people, like myself, have *chosen* to think for ourselves. This is not only a reality within the Christian church; indeed, we have heretics and those who wish to think outside the box in all the major religions, and the debate goes on.

I'M MY OWN PERSON

Pelagius suggested that *we are born perfect*. It was one of the major conflicts that Pelagius had with Augustine of Hippo, who was later elevated within the church to Saint Augustine. Pelagius argued that we are not tainted by the sin of Adam and Eve. We may share their temptations, but we are not to be blamed for the decisions they made. This makes sense to me. I am not carrying around the sins of others, and their actions and intentions are not passed down to me. I'm my own person.

Most of us have become familiar with codependency; unhealthy relationships that merge boundaries and create shame. Codependency creates blame by association. Codependents feel responsible for the actions and behaviors of others. Yet surely the sins of Adam and Eve being passed down through my mother, Maud Booth, to me is taking the codependency diagnosis to another level, and it is equally shaming.

At addiction conferences and wellness workshops, I often meet people who suffer from low self-esteem. Many have been in therapy for years trying to figure out why they don't feel good about themselves. Some suffer from depression. It affects all their relationships, and they feel uncomfortable living in their own skins.

A few have sought healing by exploring their family of origin. Did they notice similar symptoms in their parents or grandparents? Were their parents abusive? Some years ago, a movement was created for children of alcoholics—called Adult Children of Alcoholics—those who were born into abusive homes, and a number of therapeutic insights were discovered that proved most helpful in addressing the process of healing.

A NEW THERAPEUTIC MOVEMENT

It is easy to think, if you are a child growing up in a toxic or dysfunctional family, that *it is your fault*. Dad's drinking or mother's depression was caused by you. If only you had been less disruptive, received better grades at school, or been more attentive, then perhaps they wouldn't have argued or drunk alcoholically, eventually divorcing.

For therapists, the goal of establishing healthy boundaries became an essential aspect of healing the family. And, more important, it was discovered that toxic behaviors affect everyone, and therefore *all* family members need therapy. Indeed, even if the parent(s) refused treatment, the children should enter therapy for themselves.

Therapeutic Issues

Claudia Black and Sharon Wegscheider-Cruse, who were pioneers in treatment therapy for the family, began talking about the characteristics of today's adults who grew up in a toxic, abusive home. New descriptions were created that made sense. The following are some of the new descriptions.

The Hero

These children are twelve going on forty. They take over the parent role at a very young age, becoming very responsible and self-sufficient. They give the family self-worth because they look good on the outside. They are good students, excellent at sports, the prom queens, and so on. They make the family—especially the parents—look good.

When hero children become adults, they are usually rigid, controlling, and extremely judgmental of others. They achieve success on the outside but are cut off from their emotional life, their True Self. The family hero, because of their success, has the hardest time admitting that there is anything within themselves that needs to be healed.

The Scapegoat

The scapegoat child is emotionally the most honest. They express and act out the tension and anger that the family ignores. This child also provides a distraction from the real issues. The scapegoat usually has trouble in school because they get attention the only way they know how, by being negative and disruptive. They often become the pregnant or addicted teenager.

These children are usually the most sensitive and caring, feeling tremendous shame. They are born romantics who eventually become cynical and distrustful.

The Mascot

These children take responsibility for the well-being of the family. They play the role of social director or clown, diverting attention from pain and anger.

They are valued for their kind heart, generosity, and ability to listen to others. As adults, they focus on others and they rarely get their own needs met. They find it hard to receive love, creating dependents rather than friends, knowingly entering into abusive relationships to *save* the other person.

The Lost Child

These children escape by attempting to be invisible. They daydream, fantasize, read books, watch TV, or are consumed by their video games. They withdraw from reality. These children grow up to be adults who are unable to express feelings, are terrified of intimacy, and they often have relationship phobias. They socially withdraw because, in this way, they avoid being hurt.

Within the Adult Children of Alcoholics movement, family members were able to identify with these characterizations, recounting their personal stories to make these descriptions come alive. Therapists began to study and understand the complexity of tensions that existed within the family unit, giving explanations to other behaviors and attitudes that began to emerge.

Therapeutic observations helped the Adult Child understand how they became wounded within the family. It was suggested that the Adult Child had a reluctance to *talk* about what was really happening in their home; because of the toxic atmosphere within the home, they rarely *trusted* anyone and they kept their *feelings* to themselves. A new therapeutic language began to emerge that created a healing process for the whole family.

Intimacy Issues Explained

People who experienced this therapy began to understand how they developed or became involved in *needy* and *controlling* relationships. Being needy, they sought to control the situation by manipulating events so that people would stay with them. Indeed, some of these Adult Children talked about entering a world of denial, not wanting to face what was actually happening, preferring fantasy to reality.

But everything was not okay. Reality could not be ignored. Serious problems began to emerge, and many desperately asked: *Am I doomed to a life of unhappiness? Can I heal the past? Will I ever feel comfortable in my skin?*

In my book *When God Becomes a Drug*, I asked
questions like: *Are the therapists who are working
with toxic families also exploring unhealthy religious
messages that suggested we are sinful or not good
enough?* While the Adult Child was dealing with toxicity in the home, the church was teaching, as it still
does, that we all share the guilt of Adam and Eve, that
we are all damaged, tainted at birth.

I did not agree with this idea of guilt by association. Also, it is not unreasonable to suggest that the
shame people were confronting in their dysfunctional
homes should also include unhealthy religious messages they heard as children. Family of Origin issues
need to include toxic messages delivered in the name
of God. *Feelings of shame and guilt may have entered
the family through the door of religion.*

My church raised me to believe that Adam and Eve
committed the original sin that has corrupted each and
every generation. I studied the doctrine of Original Sin
at my theological college, and I was expected to teach
it, nay proclaim it, as a clergyman in the Church of
England. I remember being at a church in Darlington,
Durham, England, seeing mothers with sickly babies
rush to have them baptized for fear that they should

die and not go to heaven. These parents had been instructed to believe that baptism washed away the inherited sin of Adam and Eve. Whatever Adam and Eve's ghastly sin was, probably disobedience, rather than sex, this sin had trickled down and touched their babies in Darlington like a virus, and they needed to be cleansed, washed, and redeemed, immediately.

That was then. This is now. *I don't believe that babies are born in sin.* The God I believe in today does not hold me or anyone else responsible for the sins of another—especially sins committed in the Garden of Eden. I am responsible for my life, my mistakes, and my actions. My choice is never determined by another. *I'm my own person.*

PEOPLE MAKING MIRACULOUS CHOICES

In his disagreement with Augustine concerning Original Sin, Pelagius takes us a stage further: *A man is able, if he likes, to be without sin.*

We are free to make positive and creative choices. Yes, it is undeniably true that we can choose a behavior that produces sadness and despair, and this is often the human experience. It is our choice. However, there is also the *possibility* for us to choose something healthy, loving, beautiful, and nontoxic.

We are presented with two philosophies that are different in emphasis; we can consider the human being from the position of doom and gloom, born evil and sinful, as did Augustine or we can envision a human being, perfect from birth, divine, and actuated in their choice, like Pelagius. Are we inclined to Augustine or Pelagius? *The consequences that result from which philosophy we believe are life changing, predicating who we believe we are and the unlimited possibilities that await us.*

When we connect spirituality with the choice to take care of our bodies, when we challenge the mind in the pursuit of knowledge, seek nurturing relationships where we can honestly express our feelings, then, collectively, we are creating the spiritual bliss that Pelagius calls *perfection*.

Here are some stories that reflect how choice creates recovery, health, a loving relationship, success, and self-esteem.

* * *

In 1977, after a car crash, I received therapy for my alcoholism. I made a choice to embrace sobriety. I made a choice to involve myself in a support group, and one day at a time, I polished my ongoing recovery. I discovered a spirituality that affirms who I am, rather than what I'm not. I believe that positive thoughts produce a creative life. And I do not just believe these thoughts, I deliberately put them into action. I knew that to live a spiritual life I needed to create. I wrote books, rehearsed my appearances on television, and I even practiced telling jokes for my lectures. The point I'm making is that I contributed to my glass being full; indeed, today it's overflowing.

Do I have bad days? Sure. Do I sometimes feel like not getting out of bed, pulling the blankets over my head, and staying in the fetal position? Yes. Then I reflect on the words that Winston Churchill, when he was feeling depressed, often said to his wife, Clementine, "These dog days will not last forever."

* * *

I remember meeting Christine, who at a young age was diagnosed with depression and bipolar disorder. She knew something was wrong because for weeks she would not want to *do* anything, only stay in bed. Reading and outside activities became boring, and for months, she simply stared at the bedroom wall.

The insightful physician who diagnosed her explained that many people, including the young, had this illness. Medications were available. However, it was important for her to be surrounded by people with a positive attitude. She would need the loving support of family and friends. She had to *fight* this sickness.

Christine took her prescription drugs regularly, but she also enthusiastically embraced the prayers, meditations, and nutritious food plan offered at her spiritual center. She didn't let her sickness defeat her. Not only did she purchase uplifting books that fed her with hope, but she kept a journal to affirm a history of her progressive recovery. Today Christine is depression free and takes medication for her bipolar disorder. And as a result of her daily affirmations, she is involved in a progressive Program of Wellness.

* * *

George faced irreconcilable challenges in his first marriage and, for many months after his divorce, had battled an aching loneliness. Indeed, George realized that he had been lonely for years within his marriage. His wife, Betty, had never been interested in spirituality and so he had gone to his church and spiritual retreats alone. He had seen a therapist in the hope of healing his marriage. Slowly he came to understand that a loving marriage can never be constructed by one partner; both needed to be involved. Betty was not interested. A teenage romance had drifted into a marriage that had become a friendship. Eventually, they divorced.

George never lost hope in the possibility of a future romance. He didn't become a curmudgeon. He reflected on his personal needs, what he had to offer in a relationship, and in time discovered a wonderful woman who shared his dreams for the future. Today, George is happily married with a new family that reflects his positive spirit.

* * *

The Lam family, refugees from Vietnam, were forced to split up on their journey from chaos to freedom. They dreamed of a better life in a new world. They were forced to separately travel the high seas, facing storms, pirates, and starvation. Many refugees died in the boats.

They kept the hope alive that they would one day be united. They didn't know when or where that would happen. Some of the family eventually arrived in Hong Kong, others in the Philippines, yet others in Thailand, and, separately, they worked their way through the various bureaucratic systems of the refugee camps, always holding on to the intention that they would, one day, reconnect. After a few years of searching, they reunited as a family in America.

The Lams never lost their vision of being a family again in a different place. They believed that they would find each other. Today they live in Los Angeles, all of them pursuing the American dream, moving beyond the shadow of war into success and prosperity.

*   *   *

Alex was a teenager when he realized he was homosexual. At school and church he heard the jokes that surrounded anyone who was openly gay; he also heard his preacher proclaim that anyone who practiced homosexual abominations would go straight to hell. In spite of all he heard, Alex believed he was a child of God. He eventually came out to his family and friends, finding a different church that accepted him, a minister who nurtured him in a comprehensive understanding of the scriptures, and a community that loved him.

Today Alex is a staff member in this church, reaching out to and supporting minorities in the community.

All of the above stories reflect miraculous choices. I'm living the American dream, speaking all over the country on aspects of spirituality, as a result of the choice I made in 1977 to embrace sobriety. And the adventure continues.

Christine was told by her physician that her spiritual work helped the healing process. She made positive choices to connect with God's grace, supporting her recovery. She took her medications, embraced wellness, and found serenity in her spiritual community.

George, in spite of experiencing a loveless marriage that culminated in divorce, still wanted to have a companion. With confidence and patience he eventually attracted the right woman to share his life.

The Lam family wanted stability after the chaos of the Vietnam War and the door to that peace was their separated journey, through different refugee camps, to unite again as a family in America.

God always loved Alex; however, Alex needed to discover his own special qualities. He found within himself a genuine self-love that was reflected in personal acceptance.

AN OLD MESSAGE MADE NEW

Earlier I said that Rumi believed that the divine spirit existed *within* the human being. As he was a poet, not a theologian like Pelagius, this message is often hidden in his writings, but it's there. Of course he had many creative ideas, but he championed the concept that divinity exists within us.

I discovered something of what Pelagius is suggesting in the Rumi poem "That Lives in Us."

If you put your hands on this oar with me, they will never harm another, and they will come to find they hold everything you want.

If you put your hands on this oar with me, they would no longer lift anything to your mouth that might wound your precious land—that sacred earth that is your body.

If you put your soul against this oar with me, the power that made the universe will enter your sinew from a source not outside your limbs, but from a holy realm that lives in us.

Exuberant is existence, time a husk. When the

moment cracks open, ecstasy leaps out and devours
space; love goes mad with the blessings, like my
words give.

Why lay yourself on the torturer's rack of the
past and future? The mind that tries to shape
tomorrow beyond its capacities will find no rest.

Be kind to yourself, dear—to our innocent
follies. Forget any sounds or touch you knew that
did not help you dance. You will come to see that
all evolves us.

(From *Love Poems from God* by Daniel Ladinsky)

How can we express this transforming hope for the
future? How can we forget those things that did not
help us dance? We need to let go of the old messages.
Here are some examples:

- Religious teachings that emphasize our sinfulness
  rather than proclaim the essential divinity that
  was given to us at birth.
- Society's fearful message of *don't rock the boat*
  that kills the creative spirit.
- Parental fears that seek to protect their children
  from life's challenges, producing a dull
  conformity that suffocates individuality.

Pelagius suggests that what we were told growing up isn't necessarily true. It is okay to change our minds. Few people believe all that they heard growing up. People really do change.

EMBRACING GOD'S GRACE

What about God's grace? It's all around us. The divine energy that was given to us at birth is grace. We don't need to pray for it or beg for it; it has already been given to us. Many are unable to comprehend this concept because they are forever playing and replaying the tape that says, *We were born sinful. We were born damaged goods.*

It also needs to be said and stated clearly and emphatically that not everyone was given toxic religious messages. I know religious people who were raised in a faith where, alongside the sin message, they heard the message of God's love. Many attended uplifting services, with encouraging sermons and ministers who epitomized acceptance and hope. Today, many religious leaders are embracing a theology based upon inclusive thinking and their congregations reflect this proactive ministry. All of this is undeniably true. However, many Christians are still receiving a message that creates fear and passivity: *You are nothing without God's grace.* They are told to pray for God's salvation and grace to avoid the giant claws of Satan.

Pelagius felt that this suffocating teaching, expressed in the theology of Saint Augustine, only served to disempower human beings. Christians were passively waiting for God's grace so that they could do good works rather than activate what had been freely given. Pelagius said it this way, *Grace indeed freely discharges sins, but with the consent and choice of the believer.*

Has any human being lived the perfect life? Well, some say Jesus. Other religions may suggest their leaders. But before we get into a child's game of my ball is bigger than yours, or my bicycle is faster than yours, shouldn't we just say, "It's possible"?

INSIGHT THREE:
The Concept of Cocreation

> *"That we are able to do good is of God,*
> *but that we actually do it is of ourselves. That*
> *we are able to make a good use of speech comes*
> *from God; but that we do actually make this*
> *good use of speech proceeds from ourselves.*
> *That we are able to think a good thought*
> *comes from God, but that we actually think*
> *a good thought proceeds from ourselves."*
>
> —Pelagius's *Defense of Freedom of Will*

The powerful message that resonates in Pelagius's writings is that we play an essential part in creating the good life. Before I was reacquainted with Pelagius, I believed that *God doesn't make people good, but God wants us to be good*. This thought can also be applied to health, wealth, and success. God surely wants us to have abundance; however, He alone isn't going to make it happen. We make the moves, change the behaviors, and take the risks with

51

a willingness to walk away from what is clearly not working. The concept of cocreation is affirming that we are involved in what happens; we are cocreating *with* and *in* God.

This is not always clear when I read some metaphysical books concerning prosperity or becoming successful. Yes, it is important to tell the universe what we want (even better if we can visualize the life we want to live), but the essential piece is that we create that reality.

Over the years I've met many successful people—singers, actors, and public speakers—and the common factor that each has is the ability and willingness to work hard or think differently.

This was the essence of the debate that took place in the fourth century between Saint Augustine and Pelagius. Augustine emphasized that everything happens through God's grace; *Give me what you command and command what you will*. Pelagius felt this statement didn't address the need for human involvement. It only offered the hand that spoke of God's deliverance and ignored the hand that demands cooperation. Grace occurs when both hands are joined together to make miracle.

UNDERSTANDING MIRACLES

As a young man I thought that a miracle was something that God did, and we were amazed spectators. I've changed my mind. Today I want to emphasize our partnership with God in creating miraculous events.

There is a difference between miracle and magic. Magic is Las Vegas. We see an elephant disappear and a woman sawed in half. The next night, we see the same elephant disappear, the same woman sawed in half. Magic. Lights. Illusion. Always a trick. But a miracle is real. A miracle is not a trick, and it requires cooperation. We do something to get something.

Here are two examples from the scriptures. Virtually all of us know the story of David going against Goliath, the Philistine giant. But do we really? Let's look again.

As a young priest, I thought the essence of this story was God being on David's side against Goliath. This is only partly true, David was also on David's side.

David used skills from being a shepherd boy, and he knew what he needed to fight Goliath. He couldn't fight wearing King Saul's armor. He didn't need a sword or shield. What he needed was a sling and five smooth stones from the stream, weapons with which he had much experience. He had protected the sheep from lions and bears; his developed skills would save him from Goliath. David's selection of five *smooth* stones for a slingshot, implying a flatter stone that would glide through the air, demonstrates his involvement in this miracle. The fact that David had enough confidence in his abilities to choose the weapon he was familiar with, one that seemed impossible to be of any consequence against Goliath, instead of some other, more substantial weapon, shows that he knew himself well enough to know what to do. He was a cocreator of his choices.

Another powerful demonstration of cocreation is Jesus healing the blind man Bartimaeus. In this story, we are reminded that people who persist, in spite of great adversity, often prosper; they succeed in life. It is said that Jesus worked a miracle and healed Bartimaeus.

But what was Bartimaeus's part in creating the healing? Bartimaeus shouted. Without his persistence, the miracle would never have happened. The more he was told to be quiet, the more he shouted, "Son of David, have mercy on me!" He got Jesus's attention. Had he remained silent, sheepishly following the demands of the crowd, the miracle would never have happened.

The miracle came in the shout. His choice was the part he played in cocreation.

Here is an example of a modern miracle. Elizabeth is suffering from obesity. She has suffered with an eating disorder for many years. She is thirty-four. She decides to go to the hospital for help. She slowly begins to trust the staff at the hospital. A doctor understands her. Some counselors share with her that they also had eating disorders. She sees other patients struggling with honesty and develops a love and respect for the hospital program. She also begins to trust, which is not easy. She remembers. She cries. At times she asks, "Why?" Painful things are remembered.

At times Elizabeth feels scared. She wonders if the program is a waste of time and money. Occasionally she wants to run away.

In spite of these doubts, she continues to trust. She experiences tough love, one a day at a time. Her love and her trust grow, and she begins to listen and hear.

She can now take a compliment. She enjoys the compliments. Occasionally, she also gives compliments.

Elizabeth also hears, "We love you. We see your pain. We hear you, hear your loneliness. We love you . . . At times the disease will say to you, 'You are no good. You don't deserve all this attention.' However, the healthy side of you wants to be loved, needs the attention, and wants to share the pain and heal. The healthy side of you is the real you. . . .Elizabeth, you are a miracle. Long before the sickness began, you were God's miracle. God created you. You are God's miracle."

She hears all of these messages. This, in itself, is a miracle. She hears compliments. She begins to share her story. After years of silence, she begins to talk about her disease, about her pain, about her fatness. She explains her loneliness as a child. Her father's drunken affection. The indelicate touch. Her mother's cold glance. Constant criticism. Violence. Neglect. Isolation. Elizabeth shares all her pain.

Elizabeth learned how to eat during her childhood. Eating brought satisfaction, comfort, and relief. More eating; more comfort. Enormous eating; enormous satisfaction. She sneaked food. She hid food. Food became her protection from people. Protection from pain. Protection from criticism.

Elizabeth spoke about her understanding of religion. It told her she was a sinner, needing repentance, needing salvation. She was told that she was sinful without Jesus, without the Holy Spirit, and without the

Bible. Her fears were perceived as guilt. Being human became a sin. However, nothing was said about food. Sex was a sin, thinking about sex was dirty. Alcohol was a sin. Drugs were a sin. Nothing was said about food. It was okay to eat. Eating was good. Eating felt good.

Elizabeth was a good eater. Elizabeth's eating made her grandmother proud. Her grandmother told her that she was chubby and happy, that fat people are happy. Elizabeth wanted to stay happy, so she ate.

When Elizabeth went to visit friends, she learned how to please people. She ate all the food. All the cake. They all smiled. She once said, "No more." Everybody looked disappointed, and she wondered if she had insulted her friends. Guilt and feelings of shame resulted. She would never say "no more" again, never disappoint her grandmother or her friends. She had a distorted image of what was healthy and right.

She learned how to eat everything and vomit later. Eat and then purge. Always returning to food. Even when her anger and shame were caused by food, she would return to food. Everything revolved around food. Her sickness began to control her life, which was what made her decide to go to the hospital to seek help.

Once there, Elizabeth began to share. The disease

came alive in her spoken words. She discovered for-gotten feelings. Feelings she had swallowed, hidden, and buried with food. Elizabeth faced reality. Then she cried.

She came to see, understand, and accept the disease process. Her drug is food. Like a drinking alcoholic, she would hide it. Deny it. Lie about it. Lose her job because of it. Get divorced for it. Suffer using it. Food was her mind-altering drug. Food works. Food brings satisfaction. Food is instant escape, an addiction.

Elizabeth was not a bad, crazy, ugly, sinful, irre-sponsible girl. She was sick. She needed help. She felt she was utterly alone. In the hospital, she met fellow sufferers, people who were being treated for the same disease. The symptoms were the same, the pain the same. Growing numbers of people were demanding recognition for their disease.

The hospital helped Elizabeth treat her disease. However, Elizabeth needed to do the work, make recovery happen, and bring about the miracle. With-out Elizabeth's energy and cooperation, therapy could do nothing except give her a diet. That would be like treating a bullet wound with a bandage. Elizabeth needed more.

In order to create a realistic food program, the therapists needed honesty, willingness, and cooperation from Elizabeth. They needed to hear her stuffed feelings of fear, resentment, loneliness, and anger. They needed Elizabeth to see that in these feelings lived the disease. The food was the symptom. All the pain, all the feelings of being *less than*, all the people-pleasing had to be seen and owned. The denial, the manipulation, and the self-pity had to be seen and owned. This is treatment.

The gentle art of giving yourself permission to love yourself was introduced. Loving yourself begins when you feel your power, feel your freedom, and feel your right to choose. This is spirituality. This is miracle.

Elizabeth did not choose to have an eating disorder. She did nothing to deserve it. She certainly did not ask for it. However, she has it. That is reality. It is part of her. She can accept it, work on it, live with it a day at a time, or deny it and die. For Elizabeth to know this is to bring power, freedom, and miracle into her life. To live is to have choice. The wrong choice gives power to the disease. The right choice keeps the power with Elizabeth.

Elizabeth is free to eat destructively and die. She is

free to eat positively and live. The power and recovery rest in the feelings behind Elizabeth's eating. At whom is she eating? It is therapeutically unhealthy to bury or hide our feelings. Stuffing feelings behind food is equally unhealthy. Whatever abuse or shame Elizabeth had experienced in her life, she needs, in a safe environment, to express them. If she felt sexually abused by her father, or he was inappropriate in the way he touched her, she needs to talk about how it made her feel. Is she eating out of anger or guilt? Where is Elizabeth in her eating? If she is positive about her life, positive about her health, positive about her disease, she will choose the foods that love her. She will choose balanced food habits. She will choose to eat to live rather than live to eat. Good feelings do not require food to be experienced. Abstinence (meaning a balanced food program) must be practiced for continued recovery. Elizabeth must choose a style of eating that is good for her.

For Elizabeth, the treatment was in giving her the knowledge to discover herself, share herself, and be the creative human being she was meant to be. Today, she has discovered the creative spirituality that comes with being real. Today, she is comfortable with herself.

She is loved and loving in her new relationships. She is confident in who she is and is creating a new life and making her own world. Oh yes, she is looking and feeling healthier too.

Another miracle. People can miss the miracle of Elizabeth because they have a narrow view of God's activity. They are also in a hurry. Most miracles take time. Today, I seek out the Pelagius element in everything that I'm told is miraculous; *What is our part*?

Let's look at other examples:

We thank God that Hitler was stopped before he could kill more people. True, but let us not forget those men and women who died or suffered in the struggle against Nazism. Saying smugly that God was victorious over evil doesn't tell the full story. It doesn't include the brave individuals who contributed to the victory.

We praise God for the emerging freedom that has come to African Americans. But let us also remember to thank Dr. Martin Luther King, Jr., the freedom fighters, Rosa Parks, and others who gave their lives to achieve this God-given dignity.

In recovery circles, I often hear people say, "God got me sober." Really? What about those who do not get sober? Did God choose for them to not get sober? Also, do we really want to discount the effort of people who went into therapy and regularly attend twelve-step meetings? What is gained by discounting our part in attaining recovery?

GOD'S INTENT; OUR RESPONSE

Cocreation is restoring the balance: God's intent; our response. And because Pelagius was condemned as a heretic, we have had hundreds of years of Augustinian teaching. This teaching clearly states that God's name is to be praised and blessed, but it tragically affirms the fallenness of humanity, that we are by nature evil and are therefore sinners.

I'm looking at the prayer book I used at theological college, a gift from my mother inscribed 1966. The mindset for my prayer life was molded in this little book. These prayers would cement my codependent relationship with God for years.

Act of Contrition

I love thee with my whole heart, and I beseech thee to give me the continual increase of thy love, by directing all my thoughts, words, and actions to thy glory. Amen.

This is a beautiful prayer; however, are we seriously asking that God take over our thoughts, words, and actions by directing them? Where is the human struggle, those aspects of courage that usually precede any changes that we make? This prayer is only affirming what we want God to do. What happens if He doesn't direct my life? What happens if things get worse? Do I then blame God? Shouldn't I be doing something? Where is my involvement?

Prayer of Saint Ignatius

Teach us, good Lord, to serve thee as thou deservest; to give and not to count the cost; to fight and not to heed the wounds; to toil and not to look for rest; to labour and not to seek for any reward, save that of knowing we do thy will. Who livest and reignest, world without end. Amen.

If taken literally, this prayer would eventually exhaust or destroy a religious codependent. Surely we need balance. What is wrong with a fair day's pay for a job well done? How many people have been exploited in the workplace because of an extreme emphasis on service?

You may say I'm being unnecessarily picky, that this prayer is meant to be poetic. Yes, it is poetic for those who understand the purpose of poetry, the challenging style of allegory and metaphor. However, many take these words *literally*. Church members were raised to never question sacred writings. These prayers are revered, and those who lived them are proclaimed saints.

As we saw when we discussed Adult Children born into toxic families, unhealthy messages can create serious damage in the young and vulnerable. Indeed, a relatively new word has entered our vocabulary: dysfunction. Dysfunction is defined as "unhealthy, broken, and painfully strained." This concept should also be applied to religious messages and prayers. Our relationship with God is being reflected by these prayers, and should the thoughts and ideas be codependent, emphasizing our neediness, then the result is human impotence. The prayers and religious messages that discount our role or involvement in the activities of God, alongside the shame issues that keep us feeling sinful or like "damaged goods" combine to keep our relationship with God unhealthy.

Prayer of Saint Francis

Lord, make me an instrument of Thy peace; where there is hatred, let me sow love; where there is injury, pardon; where there is doubt, faith; where there is despair, hope; where there is darkness, light; and where there is sadness, joy. O Divine Master, grant that I may not so much seek to be consoled as to console; to be understood, as to understand; to be loved, as to love; for it is in giving that we receive, it is in pardoning that we are pardoned, and it is in dying that we are born to Eternal Life. Amen.

A part of me feared criticizing this beloved prayer attributed to St. Francis because I know how popular it is to millions of people. But it can be a setup for abuse. It is not easy to confront abusive behavior, let alone talk about it. People who are needy and fearful often put up with disparaging remarks, sometimes enduring violence from the very person they seek to please. They definitely need to speak up and establish boundaries. This prayer emphasizes passive and servile responses; the act of love and forgiveness is always directed toward somebody else. No boundaries are established that help develop self-esteem.

In theological training, these prayers were repeated weekly, if not daily, and my religious codependency was established. Pelagius challenged me to wake up and see religious codependency. We need to love God, but we also need to love ourselves. When we love ourselves, we are truly loving God.

NEW PRAYERS

The challenge facing us is enormous. The theology, philosophy, and recited prayers that we grew up with emphasize the idea that we are sinful people who are dependent upon a powerful and punishing God. *The Happy Heretic* shows how to escape from this shadow by entering into a partnership with God, affirming personal dignity alongside responsibility. New prayers, hymns, and psalms will need to be written that describe this exciting relationship.

- Instead of begging to be carried, *we walk* alongside God.
- Instead of beseeching God to grant us freedom from war, poverty, and abuse, we affirm *our struggle and perseverance,* creating peace and prosperity.
- Instead of groveling for forgiveness, *we accept* our humanness and move on, walking with our head held high.

These challenges are not stated lightly; religious traditions, teachings, and dogmas are not easily changed. I grew to love the words of the old prayers; they reflected the culture of a previous generation and the language of the Anglican Church. Even today I love to hear Psalm 23 read or sung:

The Lord is my shepherd, I shall not want.
He makes me lie down in green pastures;
He leads me beside still waters;
He restores my soul.

But what happens if the Lord doesn't lead? I do appreciate the poetry. Nevertheless, this psalm seduces me into passivity. I'm always waiting for God to make me, rescue me, heal me.

In my book *The God Game: It's Your Move*, I unknowingly wrote my Pelagian version of Psalm 23:

> *God is my friend. What more could I want?*
> *God sits with me in the quiet times of my life.*
> *God explores with me the meaning of my life.*
> *God calls me forth as a whole person.*
> *Even though I walk along paths of pain, prejudice,*
>   *hatred, and depression, my fears are quieted*
>   *because God is with me.*
> *God's words and thoughts challenge me.*
> *God causes me to be sensitive to the needs of*
>   *humankind then lifts up opportunities for*
>   *serving.*
> *God's confidence stretches me.*
> *Surely love shall be mine to share throughout my*
>   *life, and I shall be sustained by God's concern*
>   *forever.*

About the same time, I also wrote a personal prayer that celebrates my partnership with God:

Oh God, you have given me the power to
*   determine my life.*
May I remember to include myself in my amends.
May I never be afraid to reveal my anger or
*   concern to those who have abused me.*
Today I know that I can never love you or others
*   fully and healthily until I begin to love myself.*
With you as my partner and cocreator
I am discovering all that is lovable and powerful
*   within me.*
Thank you for guiding me as I reclaim myself.

These prayers are not exactly as I would write them today, but I had recognized the challenge. I sensed it was important that our prayers be proactive rather than codependent. I also knew that they were desperately needed because the old prayers beseeched an all-powerful God to intervene and remove the tribulations of his people. And if God didn't remove them— *Why has God forsaken me?*

Today I understand my partnership with God. I realize some people see me as a heretic, but I'm the Happy Heretic. I wouldn't want to go back to the old beliefs, even though I can often be found enjoying the atmosphere experienced in the ancient cathedrals of Europe. And why shouldn't I enjoy them? I would not be where I am today without the beliefs of yesterday.

INSIGHT FOUR:
Choice Is Everything

*"Moreover, the Lord of Justice wished man to
be free to act and not under compulsion;
it was for this reason that he left him
free to make his own decisions and set before him
life and death, good and evil, and he
shall be given whatever pleases him."*

—From Pelagius's letter to Demetrius

Life is a series of choices, intelligent or ignorant, and the result determines happiness or disaster. This is the essential point that Pelagius is making.

An alternative position, championed by Saint Augustine, is that God's grace alone is influencing the good choices we make, and therefore we cannot and should not take credit. It should be pointed out that Pelagius agrees that God's grace abounds, but that does not change the fact that human beings have been given the freedom to act; if they are to be condemned for the evil actions that they create, then they should be praised for their virtuous behaviors.

CHOICE CREATES SUCCESS

Let's take a relatively contemporary event and examine it:

On May 11, 1961, Rudolph Nureyev flew from Leningrad with the Kirov Ballet Company to dance in Paris. To the Russian authorities, Nureyev had already proven himself to be an individualist and a rebel. Not surprisingly, they had concerns about his even being in the West. They decided to send a telegram to Paris, demanding that he return to Moscow, supposedly to perform before the Kremlin. Instead, Nureyev placed himself into the hands of the French police and asked for protection. Seizing the opportunity of the moment, he chose to defect. The defection revealed courage. He chose to leave his family, country, and the Kirov Ballet Company for the unknown.

Nureyev was taken by the police and placed in a solitary room. He said, "Then there was silence. I was alone. Four white walls and two doors, two exits to two different lives."

In *Nureyev* by Clive Barnes, he is quoted as saying, "For me this was already a return to dignity—the right to choose, the right I cherish most of all, that of self-determination."

However, what is really interesting and speaks to the argument between Augustine and Pelagius is what Nureyev said soon after his defection: "I did not have courage to stay here—just to come and stay. I did not have courage . . . I remember I went to church, I went to Mary . . . and I said, 'Make it so that I stay without me doing it, you know, let it happen . . . without me doing it . . . that it will happen . . . arrange so that I will stay." (*Nureyev* by Clive Barnes, page 33) Nureyev was asking Mother Mary to make it happen, magically.

As I grew up reciting Anglican prayers at theological college, Nureyev was reciting Russian Orthodox prayers concerning the power of Mary. His prayers told him to go to the Queen of Heaven, and she will make miracles. But did she? It is conceivable that Mother Mary wanted Nureyev to get out of Russia, but she didn't *make* it happen. *Nureyev made it happen.*

A balanced life is when we can comfortably hold together apparent opposites: freedom and dependence, seeking God's will and doing what we think is right, trusting God and yet exercising the gift of self-determination.

THE CHURCH AND CONTROL

I ask myself these questions: Why would we want to minimize the power of choice in the living of our lives? How does it serve any religion to have millions of people pathetically dependent? What possible value is derived from such an extreme expression of religious codependency? And the answer became obvious: *control.*

If organized religion is God's sole instrument on earth, then individual choice becomes anathema. This philosophy becomes extremely powerful if we make a slight change to Saint Augustine's dictum: *Give me what (the church) commands and command what (the church) will.*

Giving complete and sole power to the church has been tragic, and the spiritual damage enormous. The legacy of rituals, prayers, and dogmas that affirm our sinfulness, unworthiness, and depravity eventually breaks the people's backbone. Some years ago John Bradshaw wrote the book *Healing the Shame That Binds You,* in which he discussed toxic shame, specifically as it relates to the family. At the same time I had written *When God Becomes a Drug,* but I hadn't comprehended Pelagius's powerful argument concerning our involvement with grace; however, I knew that some serious wounds had been inflicted in the name of God.

Christianity holds that God, in the human form of Jesus, came to bridge the alienation caused by Adam and Eve. It teaches that Jesus is the *only* means to reunite us with God, gifting us with salvation. However, it is unlikely that this was the original belief of early Christianity. It came about as a result of tremendous changes that occurred in the first three centuries involving the contemporary, social, and political climate.

The first Christians lived in a time of extreme economic, political, and religious oppression. Even during Jesus's ministry, there were differences of opinion regarding his role and intent. Some followers believed he was going to lead a political revolt, and some saw him as a spiritual leader. This difference of opinion led to many arguments and power struggles within early Christianity, and the debates still rage today.

Gradually, new interpretations of Jesus's identity and the purpose of his mission replaced the original ones. Although he had once been seen as a mere mortal, a son of man who was adopted by God, Jesus was now seen as God in human form. *God became man, and then reascended to His throne.* This gave Jesus much more power and authority and, by extension, gave that same authority to those who were called by God to speak for him, the Magisterium of the Church (the teaching authority of the church).

When it became clear that the Second Coming was not imminent, the notion of rewards, not in this life but the next, emerged. The concept of a conqueror who would physically deliver the oppressed was abandoned in favor of a Messiah who brought salvation for the next life, *if they followed the rules in this life.* This gave the church a means of maintaining control over the people without the fear of revolt.

Ultimately, this interpretation is what allowed Christianity to flourish, keeping it from being an obscure and quickly forgotten sect of Judaism At the same time, it provided a foundation for new interpretations about the source of the early church's authority. Then, when the Roman Emperor Constantine became a Christian in 312 AD, politics and religion became enmeshed. Constantine decided to unite all the people in his empire into one established religion under his authority that he shared with the bishops.

The idea that God had taken on human form in the person of Jesus and divinely appointed his disciples set the stage for the teaching that the church had divine authority. The scriptures alone were no longer authoritative; that power now rested with the bishops as Jesus's servants. *They now spoke in the name of Jesus the Christ, the Anointed One.* Later came the dogma of the pope as Christ's vicar on earth.

The changes were firmly entrenched from then on: The itinerant teacher Jesus, who referred to himself as the son of man, had been transformed into the Son of God, whose sacrifice was necessary for the salvation of the world. The message that had offered freedom for the oppressed was now used to keep them in line, if not submission.

Maybe it was during this period that the seeds of Christian guilt and shame were sown. The suffering Messiah brings a shaming message: *We were so bad that God had to sacrifice His son in order to save us.*

I believe the Christian idea of God becoming a man in the person of Jesus, of the Word becoming flesh, coming down to save the human race reinforced the idea of original sin. Today we cannot distinguish between *making* a mistake and *being* a mistake. It also conditions us to avoid taking responsibility for our behaviors. Instead we look to something (grace) or someone (God) to make us better people.

The controlling authority of the clergy was maintained by the power structure that was built into the Church, alongside the lack of education among the ordinary people. From the earliest times, the clergy was the educated class concerning the practice of religion and interpretation of the scriptures. This was true of all religions. For centuries, the general populace did not have the knowledge or skills needed to study and examine religious teachings on their own; they were totally dependent on their priests, mullahs, rabbis, monks, or shamans for guidance.

For thousands of years, human beings have been accustomed to living under an authoritarian theocracy in which the few or the chosen control the many. This divinely appointed power group claims to not only speak for God, but at times insists that it is the only way to God. Religious wars, crusades, and the persecution of heretics would follow, even into the present day.

A NEW MESSAGE

Pelagius challenged not only the teachings of Augustine but also the power structure of the early church. He proclaimed that there is a divine spirit, *spiritus*, the breath of God, in every human being, and this makes us not only special, but also *potentially* perfect.

Once his message is understood and accepted, then everything changes. We are able to interpret the scriptures for what they are, rather than make them into something they were never intended to be. We appreciate religious ministers for what they say, rather than elevate them onto pedestals beyond accountability. Also, we can respect other religions and philosophies, taking from them what will nurture and inspire our spiritual life.

The power and authority of the church came gradually. It didn't happen overnight. And the changes I'm suggesting will also take time. I'm seeing more people embracing a spiritual philosophy, questioning the teachings of original sin, and doubting an exclusive salvation promised only through the church. As I think about the power and fear that the Church hierarchy used to control millions of ordinary people for hundreds of years, I'm suddenly aware of Rumi's poem

Blood Suckers From Hell. It suggests that the poetry that celebrates passion, freedom, dance, nature, and the humor of God makes the face of orthodoxy *squint like prunes*.

Rumi speaking to a crowd muses:
Watch out for those blood suckers from hell—
    'cause they're everywhere.
And the crowd wisely retorts:
"That sounds serious—what do they look like,
    any hints; are they usually disguised?"
Rumi again: Yes, usually, they are awful tricky!
"How then to detect them?"
Well, I have noticed
their eyes will narrow and their faces begin to
    squint like prunes if they hear good poetry.

(From *Love Poems from God* by Daniel Ladinsky)

THINKING OUTSIDE THE BOX

When we exercise choice, our lives are transformed. Here is a story about a young woman who never felt comfortable with religion:

"I scared my Sunday school teachers," Anna says. "I was always way ahead of everybody. I had read the King James version of the Bible straight through a couple of times before I'd finished sixth grade."

Anna says her teachers were astonished not just that she could read the words, but that she understood the context.

"From the very beginning, I was always questioning," she says.

But one thing Anna never questioned out loud was the sexual taboos.

"I think I was in third grade when I first started hearing the phrase 'Nice girls don't do that.' I'd cringe inside, because that meant I hadn't been a nice girl since I was five years old."

Anna had been sexually abused by a neighbor at age five. The dire threats and warnings about what happens to people who "aren't nice" became her secret torment.

"I didn't dare let anybody get close to me. I couldn't let them know I wasn't nice."

As a lonely, isolated teenager, Anna often lay in bed at night, raging at God. *Why did you let that happen and then turn your back on me? It wasn't my fault. I was too little to know.*

Without having heard the words *lesbian* or *homo-sexual*, Anna knew she was different and had been all her life. She buried the secret of her sexuality, along-side her fear and guilt about the sexual abuse, under a wall of fat. "Nobody questioned why a two-hundred-and-fifty-pound woman lived alone and didn't date!"

Interestingly, Anna grew up singing in choirs and, by her own admission, remains a "musical snob" when it comes to church music: "We had a really marvelous minister of music. I think he had five music degrees. Even though we were Presbyterians, our music was more 'high church' than even the Catholic and Episco-pal churches in town."

For Anna, music was her only connection to God in church. "I'd sit there fuming at the hypocrisy of it all, but the moment the music started, I felt close to God. The most spiritual experience I ever had was when I was about twelve, and the concertmaster of the sym-phony was playing a solo. I listened to the sweetness of the violin, and the enormity of it hit me; God placed music in the world and gave us the ability to find and create beauty. I was blown away, I started to cry."

Sadly, music was Anna's only connection with God in church. Increasingly, Anna found God or serenity in other places and grew more angry and rebellious against religions that told her *where* to find God and *how sinful* she was. It was this sense of having her own understanding and beliefs discounted that drove Anna away from religion. "No matter how much I tried to tell myself that it wasn't my fault, I couldn't stop feeling dirty and worthless, especially when I really started realizing I'm a lesbian," she says. "And how dare they judge me."

Anna is slowly rebuilding her concept of God from the ground up, even though she still holds the church at arm's length. Anna says one of the biggest obstacles she faces is that some of her closest friends accuse her of not believing in God because she does not attend a church or openly discuss her relationship with God.

"Yeah, to some extent, they're right. I don't get on my knees, or read my meditation books, or any of the other things I used to do. But that doesn't mean I have no higher power, that I'm not spiritual," she says. "I just say that my God is being remodeled, and I'm still looking at designs," she laughs.

But there is a real loneliness in abandoning the spiritual accessories she had utilized throughout her life. "I tried to find a way to use them healthily," she says. "But I keep making myself wrong. I finally had to accept that I wasn't wrong. The hymns and church services didn't connect with me. I'm glad they connect with others, but they don't resonate with who I am. Music connects. Music resonates. I'm finally accepting my spiritual individuality."

This is a powerful message. What works for some people doesn't resonate with others. Also, something can work for a time until it no longer works. As a young priest I loved the rituals and theatrical ceremony in worship; today, I'm more comfortable with simplicity and silence.

SPIRITUALITY IS A CHOICE

So, if religion, for most people, is given, then spirituality, the living and demonstration of the divine experience, becomes a *choice*. We need to remember that most people are born into a religion or denomination. Our religious identity is given. Indeed, most people live and grow in the religion of their family. Spirituality is a choice. It reflects beliefs and ideas that move beyond a religion or denomination. Spirituality connects people of different religions and those with no religious beliefs. Poetically speaking, spirituality becomes the golden thread that connects humanity.

Choice is everything. We no longer wait for things to happen; *we* are now creating through choice. We know that choice involves decisions, and decisions formulate an action plan, which determines the life we live.

I've said that religion preaches what we are not; spirituality tells us who we are. For Anna, music was her connection with God; music helped her understand and accept herself. This is a *spiritual awakening*.

For years we have been told that nobody is perfect. But what if Pelagius is right, that we were born perfect and have the *potential* to remain perfect? Jesus, the saints, and holy men and women of every religion are no longer exceptions but examples. We can live like them if we make similar choices. And this does not mean that we never make mistakes or get angry or doubt our spiritual potential; indeed, it is written that Jesus occasionally lost His temper with those He considered hypocrites or the slowness of His disciples to understand His message. Jesus forcefully turned over the traders' tables inside the courtyard of the Temple; also, at times, Jesus seemed to doubt His mission on earth.

All this being said, Jesus was essentially good,

perfect in His humanness. And this is Pelagius's argument. Do not condemn every human being with the
taint of sinfulness; allow for the *possibility* of perfection in some human beings. Some men and women,
regardless of the occasional foible, truly reflect God's
divine nature.

INSIGHT FIVE:
Nature Is Good

"Moreover, the Lord of Justice wished man to be free to act and not under compulsion; it was for this reason that he left him free to make his own decisions and set before him life and death, good and evil, and he shall be given whatever pleases him."

—From Pelagius's letter to Demetrius

"Who made man's spirit? God, without a doubt. Who created the flesh? The same God, I suppose. Is the God good who created both? Nobody doubts it. Are not both good, since the good Creator made them? It must be confessed that they are. If, therefore, both the spirit is good, and the flesh is good, as made by the good Creator, how can it be that the two things should be contrary to one another?"

—From Pelagius's *On Nature*

It is amazing that a man writing in the fourth century is saying something that, even today, people do not fully appreciate: *the flesh is good*.

Why is this statement important? Because it has the potential to change many things concerning our understanding of spirituality. It also addresses some of the shame issues that spring from being human.

The idea that the flesh is good, that we were born essentially good, is another *secret* that has been kept from people for hundreds of years. Every spiritual teacher has a number of themes that they wish to emphasize in living the good life, Jesus is no exception. He warns against excessive ego and yet, at the same time, stresses a divinity that is within. "For, in fact, the kingdom of God is among you" (Luke 17:21). Jesus also indicates that his disciples can be as powerful as he is: "Very truly, I tell you, the one who believes in me will also do the works that I do and, in fact, will do greater works than these, because I am going to the Father." (John 14:12)

Is the flesh good, or has it fallen with the sins of Adam and Eve? Pelagius believed that the flesh is good: "If, therefore, both the spirit is good, and the flesh is good, as made by the good Creator, how can it be that the two good things should be contrary to one another?" This is a game changer, because now the human body is able to come out of the shadows of inherited sinfulness and finally begin to shine.

Connie Zweig and Jeremiah Abrams explained it this way in their book, *Meeting the Shadow: The Hidden Power of the Dark Side of Human Nature*:

The human body has lived for two thousand years in the shadow of Western culture. Its animal impulses, sexual passions, and decaying nature were banished to the darkness and filled with taboo by a priesthood that valued only the higher realms of spirit, mind, and rational thought. With the advent of the scientific age, the body was confirmed to be a mere sack of chemicals, a machine without a soul.

The result? The mind/body split became entrenched. . . . Like a river bed, the split runs deep in our cultural terrain, creating polarities anywhere it touches: flesh/spirit, sinful/innocent, animal/godlike, and selfish/altruistic.

We feel the terrible results of this paradigm—body as shadow—in our own lives as guilt and shame about bodily functions, a lack of spontaneity in our movements and sensations, and a chronic struggle with psychosomatic disease. The disowned body also appears starkly in today's dreadful epidemics of child abuse, sex addiction, substance abuse, and eating disorders." (page 83)

The human body was seen, in the early church, to be sinful. It was believed that the flesh, the body, indeed creation itself, needed to be restored after the fall of Adam and Eve. And it could be restored and redeemed only by the sacrifice of God's son, Jesus.

The church, alongside other religions, taught that we need to submit our thinking to the authority of the leadership, escape our physical desires and earthly feelings, and punish and control our sexual feelings, in order to experience the *illuminata* (enlightenment).

BEING REAL

I used to think spirituality was a quest to find God. Today, I believe that spirituality involves discovering me. When I discover me, I discover God working within me. This is the concept of *God within*, discovering the kingdom of God within me. The spiritual values that demonstrate God involve me.

We miss ourselves when we discount our true nature, telling ourselves we're not good enough, lacking *potential*. We miss ourselves when we don't connect with our feelings. We miss ourselves when we ignore our health or discount our physical needs. We miss ourselves if we deny the greatness of being human.

My spiritual journey includes discovering the richness of being real. I have my foibles and my challenges shaped by the circumstances of my childhood, and yet I know I'm far more acceptable to other people, and to God, when I allow myself to be real. *Indeed being real is an aspect of perfection*.

One of my favorite stories is *The Velveteen Rabbit,* by Marjory Williams because it contains many spiritual insights. One of the best insights is in the passage where the skin horse tells the velveteen rabbit about the process of becoming REAL:

"What is REAL?" asked the rabbit one day. . . . "Does it mean having things that buzz inside you and a stick-out handle?"

"Real isn't how you are made," said the skin horse.

"It's a thing that happens to you. When a child loves you for a long, long time, not just to play with, but really loves you, then you become REAL."

"Does it hurt?" asked the rabbit.

"Sometimes," said the skin horse, for he was always truthful. "When you are real, you don't mind being hurt."

"Does it happen all at once, like being wound up?" he asked, "or bit by bit?"

"It doesn't happen all at once," said the skin horse. "You BECOME. It takes a long time. That's why it doesn't happen to people who break easily or have sharp edges, or who have to be carefully kept. Generally by the time you are REAL, most of your hair has been loved off, and your eyes drop out, and you get loose in the joints and very shabby. But these things don't matter at all, because once you are REAL, you can't be ugly, except to people who don't understand."

When we are *real*, we discover our spiritual power. But more than this, when we are *real* we rediscover the perfection Pelagius spoke about years ago, the perfection of combining nature with spirit: "If, therefore, both the spirit is good, and the flesh is good, as made by the good Creator, how can it be that the two things should be contrary to one another?"

Being spiritually empowered involves allowing ourselves to be fully human, reflecting those qualities that make us unique. We become real when we give ourselves permission to think, examine ideas from different perspectives, and take responsibility for our decisions, knowing that we can always change our minds. Yes, we will have fear, and there will be areas where we are not as knowledgeable as we would like to be, but we don't let this fear prevent us from moving forward.

Many people feel spiritually empty or disconnected, even when they are active in a church or support group. *What am I doing wrong?* is a question I hear often. It's hard for some people to realize that spirituality is not something you need to go out and search for, rather it is within. Spirituality is discovering the divine presence given to us at birth.

THE OLD SPIRITUAL MODEL

Spiritual teachers often use the Body-Mind-Spirit Model to address feelings of emptiness or brokenness. The intention of this model is to bring spirituality into a *definite* connection with the body and the mind. I grew up with this model. Then I began to reflect more about what this model represented, and I became convinced that this concept, this template, *separated spirit from the body and mind*. It was doing the opposite of what it intended.

The model is usually represented by a triangle (with body, mind, and spirit at the three points) and the inside is *empty*. If nothing is inside, then God's power must be outside, and we must passively wait for God to connect or be engaged. This traditional view of spirituality teaches us to look *outward* for guidance; it feeds religious codependency and the need to be rescued or helped. It doesn't show the interaction between the connected parts of ourselves, or our interaction with God, except that we continue to ask, plead, and pray to be guided or used.

Figure 1. The Body-Mind-Spirit Model

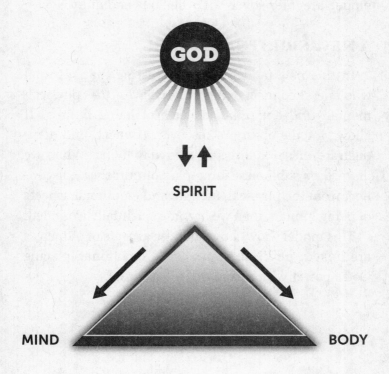

Only recently have we begun to understand how our emotions, *our feelings*, which are not discussed in this model, are interwoven with the body and mind.

A NEW SPIRITUAL MODEL

In this new model, I am suggesting that spiritual wholeness connects and interweaves the physical, mental, *and emotional* aspects of being human. It allows for the ability to discover, connect, and demonstrate these qualities in everyday living. When we discard or sublimate some part of ourselves, disconnect from the physical, mental, and emotional aspects of being human, then we become spiritually wounded.

This model shows how all three aspects of ourselves are linked: physical, mental, and emotional, placing God's power within, and it is *all* spiritual.

Figure 2. The Body-Mind-Emotion Model

God is the source of the divine energy that radiates from the core of our being. We do not need to bring something from outside; everything has already been given. In this important sense, this model reflects the unity of our physical, mental, and emotional responses. Yes, God is *transcendent*, flowing through the universe. But God's power is also *immanent*, within us. We demonstrate God's power in the healthy interconnection among body, mind, and emotions.

Rumi, in a few words, reflects this new model beautifully in his poem "Pay Homage." Here we see the power of poetry, seeing beyond theological argument into the essence of life.

If God said,
"Rumi, pay homage to everything
that has helped you enter my arms,"
there would not be one experience of my life,
not one thought, not one feeling, not one act,
 I would not bow to.

(From *Love Poems from God* by Daniel Ladinsky)

I began to develop the Body-Mind-Emotion Model after suggesting in a church sermon that we needed to pray, but we must be prepared to get off our knees and move into action. In my church, we were praying for many outreach activities, and in most cases, our involvement ended with our prayers. After the sermon, I really started thinking about the implications of what I had preached. I had paraphrased one of my favorite lessons from Dr. Martin Luther King Jr. "We should pray, but we should also be prepared to march." I now understood that entering into the march, that important physical move, was as much a prayer as the recited words. Being *prepared to march* required the willingness *to* march. Today, I understand that using the physical, mental, and emotional model reflects not only our relationship to God but our demonstration of God.

A MODEL FOR HEALTHY RELATIONSHIPS

The holistic model I have described is also powerful in its reference to relationships. It is the key to a healthy and loving connection, allowing for true intimacy.

What is necessary in any relationship is the expression of our physical, mental, and emotional natures. This speaks to the availability and interaction of the whole person as well. Romance, friendship, any relationship really, revolves around these vital components. In this way, love is expressed in a relationship. Rumi said it this way: "The one who truly loves you will set you free." Here's an example of what I mean:

A young couple rests on the grass in a park, near a lake with swans and geese. They are forever making contact, holding hands, kissing on the cheek, neck, and lips. They talk incessantly, sharing thoughts, experiences, and dreams. Family secrets and past romances are delicately touched upon, usually interrupted by laughter and smiles, occasionally accompanied by serious concentration; love is being created and demonstrated in this romantic encounter.

Walking down the path is an elderly couple. They link arms and smile at the day. How many years have they been together? Ten, twenty, maybe more. But from the manner in which they hold each other, we know that they are still in love. We are witnessing a quiet demonstration of the physical, mental, and emotional connection that has stood the test of time.

They turn and acknowledge the young couple lying on the grass. Everyone smiles. Spirituality. This story connects spirituality with love. We have heard for years that God is love. In this story, we see God's love being demonstrated, activated in the loving relationship of the elderly couple. And the young couple recognize something special; it is the awakening of a spiritual insight.

INSIGHT SIX:
We Are Created to Create

"He who hides in a napkin a talent which he
has received is condemned by the Lord
as a useless and good-for-nothing servant;
he is culpable not only to have diminished that
talent but also not to have increased it."

—From Pelagius's Letter to Demetrius

These are strong words. They reflect a parable that Jesus told his disciples: A property owner gives certain talents to individual stewards, expecting a proportionate return: "For all those who have, more will be given, and they will have abundance; but for those who have nothing, even what they have will be taken away." (Matthew 25:14–30)

This parable affirms the need to be creative, and it directly influenced the teachings of Pelagius. God has created us with a divine ingredient that enables us to create. Could it be that *this divine ingredient* is what we mean by the soul?

THE CREATIVE SOUL

You may have noticed that this book hasn't yet made reference to the *soul*. The word *soul* is known to everyone; yet what does it mean? It is not objective, like a rib or a heart. We cannot hold it or destroy it, and yet it is said to be within us. We are created with a soul. Many believe that when we die the soul moves on, journeying to heaven. Christianity and other religions talk about the soul living after death, some suggesting a stay in purgatory where it is cleansed. Most religious philosophers teach that the soul is separate from nature, our physical bodies, and so the image emerged of the body remaining in the grave and the soul traveling onward to heaven.

Pelagius does not speak at length about the soul, but he does teach that, along with our physical bodies, the soul is created perfect. Original sin, which Pelagius argued against, does not and cannot tarnish the soul. He also does not believe in the duality of the body and soul; they are one.

Interestingly enough, Rumi, in his writing called *I Seek One* suggests the same: "I am neither Christian, nor Jewish, nor Muslim. Doing away with duality, I saw the two worlds as one. I seek One, I know One, and I call One."

In this Insight, Pelagius suggests to not develop a talent made for a *good-for-nothing-servant*. He writes this because of his strong conviction that human beings have been given the power to create. As with the Creator, so with the created, we have the power to make, produce, and contribute in this world; this is *essential spirituality*. Maybe this is the soul?

The soul is that divine spark that is given to everyone, perfect in every way, as it was first received by Adam and Eve. Pelagius did not want to separate spirit from the flesh; neither was he wanting to distinguish the soul as a separate entity from the human condition, our nature. When we physically meet, I am experiencing your soul. As lovers, our souls are intertwined. Now the concept of the soul is earthed; it includes our human nature, reflecting the *whole* person.

The soul was present, although not explicitly mentioned, in the previous Insights. Now it can be fully comprehended. Nurturing the soul leads to the living of the good life (Insight One), it is perfect in every way (Insight Two), the soul enables our cocreative response with God (Insight Three), the soul is demonstrated in all our choices (Insight Four), and its nature is essentially good (Insight Five).

Unlike Augustine, who wants to separate the divine experience from the human condition, Pelagius is affirming our connection with God. In this way the soul, as a spiritual term, becomes understandable, making it a demonstrable part of who we are and what we experience.

Why did this explanation or understanding of the soul get ignored? Surely somebody connected it with the idea of the Word of God becoming flesh. If God took flesh in the person of Jesus, and we are connected with Him as the church, the Body of Christ on earth, why not connect our human nature, including our physicality, with an understanding of the soul? Well, we need to go back to those early church teachers, reflected in Saint Augustine, who said mankind and creation were fallen, sinful, and stained with the disobedience of Adam and Eve. It's hard to elevate the soul within the creature if creation is determined to be, essentially, *bad*.

Whatever God originally intended for Adam and Eve, after their disobedience, this then became the church's template of who *we* are today. Disobedient. Sinful. According to Augustine, their sin became our sin. It is this *shaming of the soul* that Pelagius argued against. He believed that human beings reflect divinity, that essential *specialness* that was seen in Jesus and other great men and women throughout history.

Indeed, if we carry within ourselves a healthy self-esteem, not arrogance, then we will create more than we were originally given, and we will share in abundance. *For all those who have, more will be given and they will have abundance.* We move away from the crippling teachings of sinfulness and become the empowered souls we were meant to be in life.

This search for essential spirituality, what I'm now calling the soul, is being tested, explored, and examined at the Institute of Noetic Sciences (IONS). A group of men and women are considering scientifically how energy, when fused together, creates such a force that it can change matter. The interrelationship of body, mind, and emotions, what I'm calling the human soul, when channeled appropriately changes the world around us.

Few realized this at the time of Pelagius, and sadly, not many appreciate this concept today. But the numbers are certainly growing and more people are open to discussing the demonstration of this divine intelligence that enables insight, healing, and transformation.

OLD MESSAGES DIE HARD

I'm writing this chapter after watching a testimony given at a televised church service. The penitent gave a powerful story based upon feeling lost and now being saved. I can't remember her exact words but to paraphrase she indicated that God is in charge. He puts people in my life that will help and support me. All I need do is follow His direction. I need to get out of my way. I need to put my thinking in a box every morning and throw away the key for that day. My thinking nearly killed me. I'm here because I'm directed by God. He is in charge. He is my Savior and He alone saved me.

The idea that we are basically worthless is still strong in many religious groups. Sadly, it can also reinforce the concept of God as the Punisher. In her wonderful book *Guilt Is the Teacher, Love Is the Lesson,* Joan Borysenko notes that the toxicity that surrounds the statement "God will get you" isn't funny when people believe it.

In her work as a therapist, Borysenko has counseled numerous people who believed God would get them or had already done so. She chronicles the case of Peter, whose critical, abusive parents raised him with an excessive Catholic fear of mortal sin. As a child, he was required to confess to his priest, who doled out harsh penances; he also had to confess to his father, who would beat him until his buttocks bled. To avoid such dual punishments, he became adept at lying, calculating how much to tell the priest so that he wouldn't appear a saint, but wouldn't be made to feel guilty.

At age forty-five, he had long considered himself an atheist, but after contracting herpes during an extramarital affair, he suffered a resurgence of his religious guilt. Catching herpes was bad enough, but the lesions always broke out on his buttocks, reminding him of his childhood agonies. Though Peter would have sworn his belief in a punishing, angry God had long been abandoned, Borysenko helped him see that he had only set them aside. She showed him that he was suffering from two cases of mistaken identity: his identification of himself as a hopeless, worthless sinner, and his understanding of God as an unforgiving punisher.

The case of Peter is an excellent example of how toxic religious messages remain firmly attached to us, hampering our ability to move away from beliefs we know have harmed us. In Peter's case, the harsh penances doled out by his priest only validated the cruel messages taught by his parents. Small wonder he could not escape his belief that God would get him, when the priest who represented God on earth stood in brutal judgment over him.

This is one of the most common forms of clergy abuse, not only the harsh penances, but the fact that a *man of God* was directing the punishment, reinforcing the unhealthy message that God is angry and vengeful. When God is used as a weapon, it is easy for people to get confused about what is actually hurting them, the weapon or the person using it. In Peter's mind, abandoning religion should have freed him from his belief that God would get him. But, as Borysenko pointed out, religion and God weren't the real problems; rather, his relationship to God was what caused his pain. In showing him that his basic beliefs about himself and God were mistaken, Borysenko opened the door that would allow him to get out of his religious prison.

Changing our perceptions about God and our relationship with God is not easy. It involves a willingness to change our beliefs. Healing toxic religious messages has brought me to think along the lines of Pelagius; we cooperate with God's grace to live the good life. And it is *essential* that we are involved in our spiritual healing.

CREATING NEW MESSAGES

With the teachings of Pelagius, we are able to examine some practical areas of our life that might require healing or change:

Personal Health

In order to create good health, we need to nurture healthy living. Do we have a nutritious food plan? Are we exercising? Do we get enough rest?

Maybe the reader is asking, "What's your point?" The point is that we need to be involved in our health. God is not codependent. If we realize the damage caused by codependency in our human relationships *then God has also got the memo*.

We are beginning to understand that we cannot make somebody happy or healthy; any relationship requires a certain detachment, a respectful space, so that the other person can take responsibility for their behavior. If we have come to understand this concerning human relationships, then it might also explain our relationship with the Divine. *God interacts with creation in a similar manner*. God will not fix our health if we continue to overeat or ignore the doctor's advice. If we eat what we like, drink what we want, and do not exercise, then we shouldn't blame God if we have health challenges. We are created to create, and we can also destroy! Here is a Pelagius-style prayer for our health:

> *God, thank you for the gift of life. Today I take responsibility for loving and nurturing this gift in a healthy way. I understand that the choices I make, the food I eat, and the rest I take will create the healthy energy I need in my life.*
>
> *I will take this prayer into action.*

Finances

I remember my mother telling me, "Leo, if you don't want to take responsibility for your money, others will step up to take care of it for you at a price."

Money is important. To waste or hide money is condemned by Jesus in the earlier parable of the talents. The landowner condemns the steward saying, "Then you ought to have invested my money with the bankers, and on my return I would have received what was my own with interest." (Matthew 25:27)

Pelagius is clear: be responsible for what is yours. It is irresponsible to say we are handing money or bills over to God. It doesn't make sense to say that God is directing our investments. Somebody who may be speaking for God or in the name of God is involved. And it could be disastrous. Here is a Pelagius-style prayer for finances:

Spirit, I am praying what I need to hear.
I'm affirming abundance rather than greed.
I shall ponder the financial advice I receive,
and then take responsibility for my actions.

Relationships

I hear people say, "God will put somebody in my life. If God wants me to meet somebody He will make it happen."

We need to become proactive and make decisions that will create a healthy relationship. Staying at home, waiting for a potential partner to come knocking on our door is a fantasy resulting in loneliness. A healthier strategy would be to reflect upon the kind of relationship we want and seek ways to bring that person into our life. Here is a Pelagius-style prayer for relationships:

Today I affirm the importance of a healthy relationship.

I reflect upon what I need in my life.
And I'm ready to go out and meet people.

Recovery Prayers

I remember hearing a powerful sentence that was attributed to C.S. Lewis, "I pray because the need flows out of me all the time, waking and sleeping. It doesn't change God; it changes me."

We have had many years of Augustinian thinking and teaching; nobody has been spared in the way it positions our relationship with God, especially in our prayers. Here are two prayers that are regularly recited at twelve-step support-group meetings:

Third-Step Prayer

God I offer myself to Thee—to build with me and to do with me as Thou wilt.

Relieve me of the bondage of self that I may better do Thy will.

Take away my difficulties that victory over them may bear witness to those I would help,
of Thy Power, Thy Love, and Thy Way of Life.
May I do Thy will always!

Seventh-Step Prayer

My Creator, I am now willing that you should have all of me, good and bad. I pray that you now remove from me every single defect of character which stands in the way of my usefulness to you and my fellows. Grant me strength, as I go out from here, to do your bidding.
Amen.

Why is all the action coming from God? Enlightened by the teachings of Pelagius, surely we need to work with God, partner alongside our Higher Power, and make changes that will support our ongoing recovery. Asking God to *take away* or *remove from me every single defect of character* is passive, emphasizing helplessness. It's also not true. I have been with recovering people for years, and I'm always inspired by their heroic acts of courage. Many went to therapy, entered recovery homes, stayed separated from family and friends, and actively changed their attitudes and behaviors with the help of the program. Our prayers need to reflect our involvement in the recovery process.

Old Prayers Made New

Let me add a Pelagius touch to these recovery prayers:

New Third-Step Prayer

I am ready to work with You in building my life.

Alongside You, I face my challenges, creating the victory I need to serve others.

May this Oneness be reflected in my life.

Amen.

New Seventh-Step Prayer

My Creator, I bring myself before You.

Working with You I seek to remove my defects of character that hinder my usefulness in this world.

Celebrating Your strength within me, I go out to do service.

Amen.

I understand and appreciate the poetic beauty of prayers, but they are dangerous if they suggest that God is doing everything. We work with God in creating the good life, one day at a time. As Rumi would say, *We Are One*.

INSIGHT SEVEN:
Change the Tape

"Nor is there any reason why it is made difficult for us to do good other than the long habit of doing wrong which has infected us from childhood and corrupted us little by little over many years and ever after holds us in bondage and slavery to itself, so that it seems somehow to have acquired the force of nature."

—From Pelagius's letter to Demetrius

It is often said that if we keep doing the same things then we'll keep getting the same results. Also, if we keep thinking the same way, we'll continue to come to the same conclusion. When we change our thinking, we change our lives.

I'm the Happy Heretic because I've created a new relationship with God that is very different from official church teaching. And this is not a problem for me; indeed I'm more comfortable in my relationship with God than I have ever been. Also, today I understand how important my involvement needs to be in affirming the good life.

Change is the operative word. We make the choice to *change* the toxic religious tape that told us we were fallen, helpless, and sinful. That shaming tape that suggested, if left to our own devices, we would amount to nothing. Only when we change this tape will we be able to demonstrate divinity in our lives.

Does changing the tape bring automatic success in every area of our life? No. We can create disaster. We can make the wrong choice, possibly resulting in failure or despair. Pelagius said *we are born perfect,* but he didn't suggest that our decisions are always perfect. We can make mistakes. We can knowingly walk away from healthy choices.

A study of history reveals heroes and villains, those who reflect perfection in life and those who seem attached to victimization and depravity. Pelagius felt that the life of perfection, or evil, is a choice. His teachings help us understand how God's grace operates in the world and what salvation can mean to Christians and non-Christians alike, even those who had lived before the coming of Jesus.

When we begin to agree with Pelagius's understanding of grace, *everything changes.* It changes how we phrase the intention in a prayer and the unlimited possibilities that we can create in our lives. And this truth has been proven throughout history. Indeed, a study of history tells us that when human beings are confronted with evil, many rise up and reflect their divine essence. The following sections offer a few examples in which toxic religion affected the lives of millions, and yet a *perfect* few confronted the thinking of the majority.

ENSLAVED PEOPLE

There was a time when slavery was pervasive throughout the world. Those who were conquered or deemed inferior were often the victims. Tragically, even today, there are parts of the world that are involved in human trafficking. However, it is slowly being exposed because of the noble actions of a few brave men and women.

The Pelagius concept that influenced these reformers was that simply praying wasn't enough. They needed to confront evil. They used every political, religious, and social argument to deliver change. Many were ostracized, placed in prison or, sadly, killed. This minority, demonstrating their *essential* divinity that

I have called the soul, eventually forced changes in society.

It is hard to believe that a forceful endorsement for slavery was based upon the scriptures. It was argued that the descendants of Ham were black Africans, and they were cursed by Noah, the father of Ham, to become the lowest of slaves.

And Ham, the father of Canaan, saw the nakedness of his father, and told his brothers outside. Then Shem and Japheth took a garment, laid it on both their shoulders, and walked backward and covered the nakedness of their father; their faces were turned away, and they did not see their father's nakedness. When Noah awoke from his wine and knew what the youngest son had done to him, he said, "Cursed be Canaan; lowest of slaves shall he be to his brothers." (Genesis 9:22– 25)

In early Christian writings we see that slavery is permitted with the admonition that the owners be kind! *Masters, treat your slaves justly and fairly, for*

you know that you also have a Master in heaven.
(Colossians 4:1) *Slaves, accept the authority of your*
masters with all deference, not only those who are kind
and gentle but also those who are harsh. (1 Peter 2:18)

We've discussed earlier how the Augustinian
teachings became the authoritative teaching of the
church, and because slavery was supported by most
bishops and clergy, who spoke in the name of God,
then ordinary people accepted that slavery was part of
the Divine Order. Indeed, some slaves believed this.

Slavery went alongside rampant racism; those in
the civil rights movement often discussed both issues
in the same sentence. Nobody did more to expose the
bigotry of slavery and racism than Dr. Martin Luther
King Jr. Here is an excerpt from one of his sermons
called, "Our God Is Able" from 1956 in Montgomery,
Alabama. Although Dr. King was not a Pelagian, he
knew that people needed to rise up, get involved, and
confront this evil.

In our own nation, another unjust and evil sys-
tem known as slavery, for nearly one hundred
years inflicted black people with a sense of

inferiority, deprived them of their personhood, and denied them their God-given rights of life, liberty, and the pursuit of happiness. Slavery was the shame of America. But as on the world scale, so in our nation, the wind of change began to blow. One event followed another to bring an end to slavery and the system of segregation that was created in its aftermath. Once, long ago, people justified slavery by quoting the scriptures; today we know with certainty that discrimination and racism are wrong. The only question remaining is how long their pernicious effects will continue to cripple our democracy.

These great changes are not mere political and sociological shifts. They represent the passing of systems that were born in injustice, nurtured in inequality, and reared in exploitation. They represent the inevitable decay of any system based upon principles that are not in harmony with the moral laws of the universe. When, in future generations, people look back upon these turbulent, tension-packed days, they will see God working through history for our salvation. They will see that God is able to conquer the evils of history.

But more than this, they will see how any change that overcomes evil requires *our involvement*. History records that it is people who confront abuse and discrimination; people challenge toxic teachings; it is people that enhance and make our society a better place to live in.

Yes, God is involved, but for change to occur, we need to be involved.

SUBJUGATED WOMEN

The church's attitude concerning the role of women has been inconsistent. Eve was blamed for Adam's fall from grace, and yet Mother Mary is seen as the vehicle of salvation. As with slavery, selected scriptures have not been helpful. Notice how the quotes found in Genesis are later used in the Christian letter of Timothy to justify the teaching that a woman should remain silent and submit to the authority of a man.

And the rib that the Lord God had taken from the

man he made into a woman and brought her to the man. (Genesis 2:22)

So when the woman saw that the tree was good for food, and that it was a delight to the eyes, and that the tree was to be desired to make one wise, she took of its fruit and ate; and she also gave some to her husband, who was with her, and he ate. (Genesis 3:6)

Let a woman learn in silence with full submission. I permit no woman to teach or to have authority over a man; she is to keep silent. For Adam was formed first, then Eve; and Adam was not deceived, but the woman was deceived and became a transgressor. Yet she will be saved through childbearing, provided they continue in faith and love and holiness, with modesty. (1Timothy 2:11–15)

Some theologians have argued that women should remain submissive and are not equal in regard to performing certain sacraments. A possible example might be seen in officiating at the Eucharist or being ordained priests in the Roman Catholic Church.

A few Christian husbands expect their wives to obey them because they believe God has placed husbands in authority over any wife. With manipulation of the scriptures, this has led to sexual exploitation, domestic violence, and a comprehensive dismissal of the role of femininity in the religious life.

This wrong is being addressed. Most churches today have removed language from their rituals and ceremonies that make women vulnerable to abuse and exploitation. Today, women are ministers, priests, and bishops in non–Roman Catholic Christian denominations; books are being written about the divine feminine, and women are affirmed as essential players in the religious life. Change is happening.

CONDEMNATION OF SCIENTISTS

Lastly, let's consider the disagreements that occurred between Galileo and the church around the year 1610 AD. Galileo, considered by many to be the father of science, championed the work of Copernicus, which placed the sun at the center of the universe, challenging the teaching of the church, which said the Earth is at the center of the universe. The church used Psalm 96:10 to justify its teachings:

Say among the nations, "The Lord is king!
The world is firmly established; it shall never
   be moved."

The church immediately condemned the science of Copernicus and Galileo, which today is accepted by scientists. Galileo was judged and placed under house arrest for the rest of his life. He died in 1642. The Inquisition's ban on reprinting the words of Galileo was lifted in 1718, and the Catholic Church only acknowledged its *mistake* in 1992, twenty-three years after man first landed on the moon!

Today science is not seen as the enemy. Most Christians and members of other religions see God at work in both science and medicine. These disciplines only make our understanding of the universe even more miraculous.

A HEALTHY TAPE

We grow and learn when we willingly enter the process of change. It's tragic to resist it. Let's review some of Pelagius's insights to help us erase some religious tapes that are no longer helpful.

A significant argument is that everyone is born perfect. This reflects Pelagius's belief that what was good at the beginning of creation, in the Garden of Eden, holds true for every child who is born. The essential goodness of God is forever being reflected in creation. *Original Sin is replaced by Original Perfection.*

In the book *The Varieties of Religious Experience*, William James quoted from a letter written by the eminent Unitarian minister Edward Everett Hale:

> *A child who is early taught that he is God's child, that he may live and move and have his being in God, and that he has, therefore, infinite strength at hand for the conquering of any difficulty, will take life more easily, and probably will make more of it, than the one who is told that he is born the child of wrath and wholly incapable of good. (page 83)*

This Insight changes not only our relationship with God but also our relationship with the church and ourselves. God's grace cannot be manipulated by the sacrament of baptism; God's grace is freely bestowed upon every child, whether baptized or not. The sin of Adam and Eve remains with Adam and Eve; it is not passed down from one generation to another. Adam and Eve were responsible for their lives; we are responsible for ours.

Pelagius's words: "The God I believe in today does not hold me or anyone else responsible for the sins of another; not even sins committed in the Garden of Eden."

Another Pelagius insight concerns the divine gift of choice: "A man is able, if he likes, to be without sin." This is the most challenging teaching to accept. Why? Because for hundreds of years we have been told that we were sinful, damaged, and unworthy. It's not easy to change this mind-set. However, if we can view Jesus not as the exception but rather the example then maybe it is *possible*. Jesus is what we can be!

Blasphemy! Heresy!

Well, yes, if we are following the dictates of traditional dogma. But if we give ourselves permission to think differently and reflect upon the implications of what Pelagius is saying, then it might make sense. Isn't this what we did with arguments concerning slavery, women, and the science of Galileo?

And maybe this is why we need poets, why we need Rumi. He argues against rigidity, formality, and rules that either don't make sense or are not working. And in his humor we discover a truth. Consider his poem "Hey."

> The grass beneath a tree is content and silent.
> A squirrel holds an acorn in its praying hands,
> offering thanks, it looks like.
> The nut tastes sweet; I bet the prayer spiced it
>   up somehow.
> The broken shells fall on the grass,
> and the grass looks up and says,
> "Hey."
> And the squirrel looks down and says,
> "Hey."
> I have been saying "Hey" lately too, to God.
> Formalities just weren't working.

(From *Love Poems from God* by Daniel Ladinsky)

I realize it's always dangerous to quote a scriptural text or take a saying attributed to Jesus and build a theory; however, when Jesus says, *I came that they may have life, and have it abundantly* (John 10:10), what is the message? Surely it is more than an affirmation concerning abundance. Doesn't it speak to a creative life based upon the *experience* of knowing Jesus and, more importantly, *demonstrating* divine virtues? We have the *possibility* of being more. The anointing that Jesus received, he shares with *everyone*.

What are the chances of remaining perfect all our lives? Pelagius himself admits, very small. But there is a chance; a possibility. I'm dancing with Pelagius and Rumi when I allow myself to consider unlimited possibilities.

A friend said recently, "Leo, I need to move away from the sin-syndrome." Absolutely. An overemphasis upon sin and unworthiness eventually creates disempowerment. We manifest what we believe. What we say and think about ourselves, we will demonstrate in our lives. This includes our understanding of God.

A view of God as the Rescuer or Punisher has a direct effect on how we live. Remember, historically, religion has told us what we are not; rarely did it explicitly tell us who we are.

Some may still ask, "What is the point, then, of God's grace? Haven't you got rid of it?"

No. And I don't believe that Pelagius discounted God's grace. On the contrary, we cooperate with God's